D1474964

Books by Allan Keller

Scandalous Lady   *1981*

The Mill at Phillipsbury Manor
(with charles howell)   *1977*

Life Along the Hudson   *1976*

Colonial America   *1971*

The Spanish-American War   *1969*

Morgan's Raid   *1961*

Thunder at Harper's Ferry   *1958*

Grandma's Cooking   *1955*

Madami (with anne putnam)   *1954*

SCANDALOUS LADY

SCANDALOUS LADY

The Life and Times of
MADAME RESTELL,
New York's Most Notorious Abortionist

ALLAN KELLER

ATHENEUM 1981 NEW YORK

Library of Congress Cataloging in Publication Data

Keller, Allan.
Scandalous lady.
Bibliography: p.
1. Abortion—New York (N.Y.)—History—19th century.
2. Restell, Madame, 1812–1878. 3. New York (N.Y.)—
Social conditions. I. Title.
HQ767.5.U5K44 1981   363.4'6'0924   18–66088
ISBN 0–689–11213–0   AACR2

Published simultaneously in Canada by McClelland
and Stewart Ltd.
Composition by American–Stratford Graphic Services,
Brattleboro, Vermont
Manufactured by R. R. Donnelley & Sons Co.,
Harrisonburg, Virginia
Designed by Mary Cregan
First Edition

*To my daughters
Barbara and Katharine
who understand*

ILLUSTRATIONS

SCANDALOUS LADY

PROLOGUE

It was no night to be out without urgent reason. Snow swirled through the streets of mid-Manhattan, driven by a bitter wind that piled drifts under the steps of brownstone houses and against the buildings. Gaslights at street intersections cast a sickly glow that hardly penetrated the dark of night at the base of the poles.

A church clock struck twice from a belfry on a side street and a policeman, helmet held on by a heavy woolen scarf, trudged up Fifth Avenue patiently, thinking ahead to relief at four o'clock. He had barely been swallowed up in the eddying snow at 52nd Street when a hansom cab appeared as if by magic from out of the storm and halted at the side entrance of the mansion on the northeast corner of the intersection of street and avenue.

The driver of the cab, bundled to the throat in a greatcoat and buffalo robe, remained perched on his high seat as an elderly man stepped from the hansom, turned, and assisted a woman to alight. She was attired in a warm coat, which was covered in turn by a long cape that concealed her from her bonnet to her toes. A heavy veil hid her features so completely that, if a passerby had happened to walk past, he could not have told whether she was large or small, old or young, black or white, sinfully ugly or ravishingly beautiful.

The woman appeared to stumble, perhaps from the slippery condition of the sidewalk, but her escort's arm steadied her. They crossed to a small iron gate in a railing surrounding a tiny yard, opened it, and went in to a rear door. There was no visible light in the big, four-story dwelling but just as the two reached the entrance, it was opened from inside, a shaft of yellow light flickered in the snow, and they passed in out of the storm.

Twenty minutes later the man emerged as silently as he had entered, stepped into the hansom, and was driven away. Within moments the footprints of the man and woman had been obliterated, as if the couple had never been there at all.

Three nights later, at almost the same hour, the hansom cab drove up to the side entrance of the mansion again and the same man entered the house. The storm was over, but darkness cloaked 52nd Street, turning it into a mysterious place where there was truly no darkness and light, but only dark shadows and lighter shadows. This time, when the couple emerged from the silent, unlighted house, the woman clung desperately to her companion, and had to be lifted into the hansom cab. For a while there was only the clip-clop of the horse's hooves in what was left of the snow, and then that too died away in the night.

Neighbors of the tenant in the brownstone house could have surmised what went on behind the drawn blinds and lowered shades of that elegant residence on Fifth Avenue. Sometime during the three days and nights—probably soon after the woman's arrival—she had submitted to an illegal abortion. Without doctor or nurse in attendance, a miscarriage had been induced by the most notorious abortionist in New York's history.

The young woman in the long cape and the dark veil—who was she? It really does not matter, for her name was legion. She may have been the daughter of one of the city's finest families. The hansom cab and liveried driver would suggest this. But it may have been only a hired carriage, and the woman a desperate victim whose father had scraped together enough money to pay for the expensive operation.

The time was the 1870s, near the end of the three decades or more during which Mme. Restell had done her work in three successive "offices" as she rose in wealth and fame—and notoriety. This last place of business and residence combined was a veritable gem of a home, set among other lovely stones in the tiara of residences that graced upper Fifth Avenue.

The casual observer would never have dreamed that it was the lair of an abortionist, that night after night frightened women hastened through the side entrance to be freed of the social stigma of bearing an illegitimate child or the financial burden of having a legitimate but unwanted baby.

In an era of titans with names such as Astor, Vanderbilt, Gould, and Harriman, the owner of the dwelling was a famous figure in her own right. Despised by some, blessed by others, and tolerated by most, she played a role applauded in secret by untold thousands of women, women still waiting for their own freedom in an era of male ascendancy.

AN ARRIVAL
FROM ENGLAND

They called her "Madame Killer" behind her back and gawked at her when she rode up Fifth Avenue behind a pair of matched grays for a pleasant drive in Central Park. Two men attired in black livery with plum-colored facing on the coat lapels rode on the seat ahead of her, one holding the reins and the other appearing to be in a crouching position, so eager was he to jump down and assist his employer if she interrupted her outing to do a little shopping.

Her dressmaker must have been one of the best in town. She had turned out the lady in the carriage as the very picture of high fashion: bombazine dress barely revealing high-buttoned shoes, a wasp-waisted coat of fine woolen cloth trimmed in mink, and a bonnet tied under the chin. She had made a small muff of mink in which the lady in the carriage hid her hands, much like those famous pianists or violinists used to protect their hands from harm.

Many of those on the sidewalk knew the lady by reputation and marveled at her sangfroid. There were others who knew her better—much, much better—and these watchers, most of them fashionably dressed women, shivered despite their efforts to appear unconcerned, or found themselves breaking out in a clammy sweat.

"Madame Killer," whom the police of New York knew as Mme. Restell, was the best-known abortionist in the city but few officials wanted to tangle with her. They were wise to arrive at this decision for the lady—who hardly deserved the title—had threatened again and again to bare some of the fanciest skeletons in New York society if anyone had the temerity to bother her.

By this time in her career she could boast of an income in six figures, the more to be remarked upon because the nation was in the depths of a serious depression. Rumormongers said she had a heart of granite. It was a judgment without any evidence. Very few knew her well enough to know her character or thoughts. She, like the poor, the hungry, the jobless, and those more fortunate at the moment, was a product of her times.

The people in the breadlines had pawned their overcoats, and many a man had neither socks nor overshoes to protect his feet from the icy pavement as he waited for a chance at a morsel of food. The poor people had taken to sneaking into the better neighborhoods in the small hours of the morning to spill garbage out of the wooden barrels. They had a two-fold purpose: to find something edible and to knock the barrels apart for use as firewood.

For one of those reasons only politicians understand, government officials refused to call it a depression but the people in New York knew better. Young boys and girls by the thousands, homeless and penniless, roamed the streets and huddled together in doorways and alleys to keep warm. Vice was sold so cheaply on the streets that the madams of houses of ill repute were frequent visitors at the precinct houses, complaining to the police that they would have to reduce their payments for protection if something was not done.

There was not much the constabulary could do, so busy were they trying to reduce crime. The alleys in the blocks running off Fifth Avenue above 34th Street were usurped at night by roving gangs of footpads who pulled men into the dark recesses to rob them of their wallets and outer garments. A century later these victims would have been knifed or bludgeoned, but in those unsophisticated days just enough force was used to gain the necessary end.

Mme. Restell's business flourished despite the economic troubles that beset her neighbors. Other residents in the handsome brownstone fronts on Fifth Avenue might be concerned about Jay Gould's and Jim Fisk's financial maneuverings, but not the owner of the mansion on the corner of the avenue at 52nd Street, where in good and hard times alike there was a continuing need for a certain professional expertise. Young women, both of high and of low station, had a propensity for getting into trouble. When this happened, Mme. Restell was the only person in whom most of them dared to confide.

Her neighbors—even those most alarmed by the decline in value of their stocks and bonds—reserved enough time from their worrying to plot schemes to get Mme. Restell to sell her house and move away. Nothing had succeeded so far. Many of the social elite had recently moved to the upper avenue from Murray Hill and other areas south of 34th Street, annoyingly forced to do so by the steady uptown march of commercialism, only to discover that the fine house on the desirable corner was the dwelling place and "office" of the city's most expensive and successful abortionist.

There were ugly rumors bruited about, supported by

occasional glimpses of a hearse backed up to the side entrance. The men who witnessed this telltale sight, usually when they were returning from a late night at the club, might have considered it evidence enough to justify a visit to the district attorney's; but having heard of Mme. Restell's threats to open some of the most scandalous closets in town, they never took the step.

Fear was not the only shield protecting Mme. Restell. Many New Yorkers viewed her not as an evil presence but a necessary evil. She was, in a way, a victim of the times, in a society that refused to face the facts of life and employed the abortionist as an escape valve for its own sins. Mme. Restell could not have existed a month if the people had not wanted her there.

As a matter of cold truth, the fashionable woman who conceived an illicit lover's child could claim no moral superiority over the abortionist, but could use her to rid herself of the evidence of shame while appearing to be above reproach. Perhaps it was a cowardly thing to do, but it was forced upon the unfortunate woman by the existing moral duplicity.

Before the Civil War Mme. Restell's life had been different, at least outwardly. She had not achieved the kind of fame that engendered financial success and the power to hold the authorities at bay. There had even been a time when mobs ran through the streets thirsting for her blood and threatening to burn down the humbler lodgings she owned downtown.

But the fratricidal Civil War had fostered a more relaxed emotional climate. When men were dying by the thousands the crimes of one abortionist seemed unimportant. Then, in the years of Reconstruction and westward expansion that followed, one woman's behavior was lost in the general excitement.

Her knowledge that she was no worse than many of the women who used her services made it possible for her to glory in her affluence and in the secret weapon she held, a weapon that terrified women by the hundreds and their paramours as well. When she went out in the town it was sheer bravado. There was no skulking on side streets or hiding in the dark. She saw no reason to stay behind the shuttered windows of her house. She seemed almost to be daring her enemies to do something.

This remarkable woman was born Anna Trow in the little hamlet of Painswick, England. She arrived there in 1812, the very year when England made her last futile attempt to recoup the loss of her American colonies. Painswick was one of those English villages—it was in Gloucestershire—depicted so often on postcards or on slides prepared for a traveler's lecture. Quaint and pretty is the best phrase for it, with thatch-roofed cottages, an ivy-clothed church, and a tavern in the center of the hamlet.

Anna's father was a farm laborer, than which there was nothing lower in the social scale, unless it was a gaolbird or a highwayman. At that, the highwayman was considered more of a success, and much more glamorous—at least until he landed on the gibbet. As the girl grew up she had to make her own way, and when the boredom of household chores and other menial tasks brought her nothing but disillusionment, she turned to marriage as an escape. Her husband was Henry Sommers, the village tailor, and he must have possessed some slight aura of glamour to appeal to a girl in her late teens.

Before the honeymoon was over both of them realized that England held little promise for them. Stuffing their few belongings into a bag or two, they emigrated to the United States, landing in New York in 1831. The city differed greatly from Painswick, but it too boasted an exterior that hid unsanitary arrangements, wretched housing for the poor, and working conditions that demeaned employee and employer alike. Most of the city was compressed within the lower part of Manhattan Island, south of 23rd Street, but various shantytowns existed elsewhere on the island. In some sections the sewers were open ditches alongside the streets, in which pigs rooted and chickens scratched. Outhouses stood behind all but the very finest houses, and disease was both endemic and epidemic.

There is no record to show how the young immigrant prospered at his trade or where the couple lived. The first definitive word of their life in the new world had nothing to do with life at all—or perhaps everything. It was a notice that Henry Sommers died of typhoid fever in 1833, leaving Anna with a small child. She must have stayed a widow for at least two years. This assumption is based upon the fact that she took for her second husband one Charles Lohman, described as a printer on the *New York Herald*. James Gordon Bennett, the elder, founded the *Herald* in 1835, two years after Henry Sommers's demise.

One wonders how the young widow supported herself and her baby during the interval. There is some indication that she practiced midwifery, perhaps with occasional ventures into less respectable sidelines, because she and the newspaper printer had barely been married before they began advertising the woman's accomplishments in the city's journals. They were small, discreet notices, tucked away inside the pages with auction notices, announcements of bargains in the dry goods stores, and word of the availability of such tradesmen as harness makers, blacksmiths, wheelwrights, and tinsmiths. The advertisement usually ran like this:

> Madame Restell, the female physi-
> cian, is daily at her office, No. 146
> Greenwich Street, where she will
> treat diseases to which females are
> liable.

No one knows where she picked up the nom de crime of Madame Restell. To the ears of the English-born woman it may have sounded more pleasant—and more fashionable —than Lohman, or she may have had a simpler motive: the desire to keep her legal name from being bandied about in the streets.

At times the notices in the advertising columns were more expansive, boasting of her many years of experience, her great success in dealing with women's troubles, and less frequently, guaranteeing "a cure at a single interview." Again and again there was mention of her "infallible French female pills."

A busy corner at Greenwich Street, painted in 1810, not long before Madame Restell took up residence there.

There is nothing in the history of medicine to support the myth that the French knew more about the various ills of women than any other nationality, but in the decades when America was young there was no scotching the widely held belief. What is clear is that Mme. Restell had touched a key which brought instant and remunerative response. Women flocked to her small house, which was then in a middle-class residential district of one- and two-story frame dwellings. Some wanted only advice on their approaching accouchements or actual help at the time of delivery, but more of those who hurried to her office wanted their pregnancies terminated. Of the latter, those who were lucky had miscarriages brought on by powerful drugs concocted in the back room and sold as the "infallible French pills." Those not so fortunate had but two choices: either the birth of an illegitimate child with its resulting scandal or recourse to mechanically induced abortion.

Just why married women sought Mme. Restell's legitimate services is readily apparent when the mores of the times are taken into account. Young American mothers considered it unutterably immodest for a male physician to attend them during pregnancy or at their delivery. Many of those who did call in male doctors insisted that they be examined under a sheet, and even that their babies be delivered under cover and out of sight of the attendant. This false modesty and highly cultivated innocence led to the employment of many midwives, often of foreign birth and training and of indifferent intelligence and cleanliness. Childbed fever was just one of the results of this slipshod care.

Whatever Mme. Restell made as a midwife was dwarfed by her earnings as an abortionist. If she asked too much to deliver a baby the mother-to-be could seek other midwives or risk having the baby at home with no one to help in the delivery except the husband. But when a pregnant woman with an unwanted child—a child that would doom her to everlasting scandal and shame—dealt with Mme. Restell at 146 Greenwich Street, she was hardly able to exert much pressure for a low fee. Then, too, Anna's own danger, that of being apprehended and imprisoned for criminal abortion, was so great that she had to insist on large fees, hoping to make enough to retire, as well as to pay for bail bonds and bribes to the authorities.

Added to her other income was rent paid by some women who did not want an abortion but did not wish the world to know about the birth of an illegitimate child. Mme. Restell, in truth, ran what resembled the reputable institutions sponsored many years later by private welfare organizations. These women in trouble were wealthy, for the most part, and their families sent their daughters off to "travel for their health" or "to visit relatives" whose homes were invariably at a great distance from their own. Instead of sailing abroad to foreign watering places or going to American spas, or looking up nonexistent relatives in faraway states, these young women made their clandestine way downtown late at night and entered Mme. Restell's establishment, there to remain until the baby was delivered and they themselves well recovered. A few of these women took their babies home with them, to be foisted off as the legitimate offspring of relatives or servants, but most of them made terms with the abortionist to have the infants "adopted out." When these babies were turned over to barren couples the lady on Greenwich Street pocketed additional fees. She had an amazing way of making money out of every variety of human longing, fear, and remorse.

Though she was obviously amoral by profession, there

must have been decency in her. She cared well for the women who did want their babies delivered in good health. and she was said to have removed her own child from the scene of her activities. There is nothing to show where this child was during all the years when Mme. Restell was building her reputation, but we do know that the child made the practitioner of Greenwich Street a grandmother. When that happened Anna proved to be a most sentimental, even maudlin, grandparent.

Life being what it is in a city, the goings-on in the house near where the American Stock Exchange now stands could not be expected to escape notice. Neighbors saw women coming and going, mostly at night, and realized that the owner of 146 Greenwich Street was engaged in a most questionable business. Some of them protested in person. The "female doctor" would then assure them that she was only doing what any decent physician would do: caring for mothers-to-be. This did not satisfy the observant, who could do simple addition and subtraction.

Spurred on by their suspicions, the neighbors held secret meetings at one another's homes, sought ways to persuade Mme. Restell to move away, and when that failed, formed a vigilante committee. Each night members of the group took turns spying on the "physician's" house, trying to learn more about her secret practice.

Snug inside her establishment, Mme. Restell would not have been human had she not chuckled at the discomfort she was causing her neighbors. Her section of town was exposed to the bitter, icy winds that blew across the Hudson from the Jersey meadows in the winter. They swept up the narrow streets between the buildings, and as her house was but two very short blocks from the river, at or near the corner of Liberty and Greenwich Streets, the self-appointed guardians of the law spent many a cold night at their task.

What the policemen walking their beats thought of all this has not been recorded. It can be surmised that the police then, as now, looked with a jaundiced attitude upon civilians playing spy, or pretending to be members of the watch and ward societies. The blue-coated officers undoubtedly knew precisely what was going on at the Restell place, but who were they to interfere when the newspapers and magazines were carrying advertisements blatantly offering the same services as Mme. Restell did, acting as shills for the many operators offering relief from "women's ills"?

The average policeman has always looked at things with a degree of fairness. If women in trouble were not prosecuted, why should Mme. Restell be? If she was in the wrong, let the board of aldermen and the mayor put a stop to it. Was not her service as legitimate as the nostrums touted in the papers, things like Dr. Scott's electric flesh brush and Dr. Owen's body battery? The first, said the ad, "opens the pores, beautifies the skin, and allows the body to throw off impurities. It cures: sciatica, rheumatism, gout, lumbago, toothache, and quickly removes those backaches peculiar to LADIES." The secret of its power, the promoters averred, is that "The Germ of all Life is Electricity." Dr. Owen's magic belt and battery, it was claimed, "contains 10 degrees of strength. Current can be applied to any part of the body and cures general nervous and chronic diseases." There were pills to restore manly vigor and womanly appeal, cure what the French called the English disease and the English called the French disease, positively end baldness, and perform 101 other wonders. Why bother, then, about a woman who claimed only to cure the ills common to women?

As it happened, it was neither the nosy neighbors nor the police who first brought to public notice proof that Mme. Restell was actually engaged in illegal business. A young woman walked into City Hall one blustery February day, sought out Mayor William F. Havemeyer, and lodged a complaint against the female "physician." She was Mary Applegate, a Philadelphia girl just out of her teens, and she admitted that she had loved not wisely, but too well. Finding herself pregnant, she had confessed to her parents and subsequently had hidden herself away in Mme. Restell's establishment to await the birth of her child. Having decided to bear the child, she had no fear of anything other than detection, and as she had no friends or relatives in New York, her anonymity seemed assured. Her delivery had been devoid of complications, she told Mayor Havemeyer, but several days after her baby's birth the child had disappeared.

"I have been an inmate of Mme. Restell's house for some time," she wept. "I have been unfortunate, as you may suppose, Sir, or I would not have been in such a place. But what I want is my baby! I don't know where it is or what she has done with it."

The "Applegate woman" signed an affidavit and a warrant was sworn out for the "physician's" arrest. Mme. Restell was hauled off to jail to await a hearing.

This was all a certain segment of the city's population needed. Excitement rose to a noisy peak, people stormed into the streets demanding severe punishment for the accused, and whatever secrecy Mary Applegate had sought was destroyed in headlines across the pages of all the papers. A mass meeting was held in a hall on Cortlandt

Street, where local pastors and other speakers incited the gathering to take matters into its own hands. The mob burst from the meeting house and rushed down the street toward the corner of Greenwich and Liberty Streets screaming for action.

"Burn the house down over her head," some shouted. "Search the house," screamed others. "How many babies are buried there?"

A platoon of fifty policemen arrived just ahead of the vanguard of the mob. The bluecoats formed ranks at the steps and stood off the angry citizens. There was considerable violence, as the police were not the only ones carrying clubs, but things quieted down when five men were arrested and carted off in a paddy wagon.

The next day there was a story in one of the dailies alleging that the rioting had been instigated by a man who had been blackmailing Mme. Restell and was angered when the woman "physician" refused to pay any further hush money.

When the case reached the courts Mme. Restell said she had put the baby out for adoption and that a woman from the Middle West had taken it. There were charges and countercharges having to do with whether the Restell woman paid various officials to drop the matter or if she had threatened to air a few secrets. When the dust cleared, the lady "physician" went back to her office, free of any legal charges, but with the lasting enmity of thousands of New Yorkers. One strange fact is that some of these women had themselves been clients of the abortionist.

It was not the end of the incident by any means. Mary Applegate, although chastened by the notoriety, still wanted her baby in her arms. Her sorrow darkened her Philadelphia home until her father, seeking to help her, traveled to New York to ask Mme. Restell for leads to the baby's whereabouts.

Not wanting to lose the adoption fee she had obtained for handing over Mary's illegitimate child, Mme. Restell agreed to give Applegate the adoptive mother's name for $5,000. He gave the abortionist the money and obtained the name of a woman whose trail led to Cincinnati, but there it was lost. The child was never recovered.

Mme. Restell had had a narrow escape—both from the law and from the mob—but she had turned a pretty profit in the deal. First she had pocketed rent from the unwed mother while waiting out the pregnancy. Then she had obtained a fee for the delivery. Next she was paid for providing the other woman with a child, and finally she hit the jackpot with the $5,000 bribe for giving information that did no one any good.

MME. RESTELL AND
NEW YORK
SUITED EACH OTHER

The young "female physician" had come through this incident without harm. Her coolness and her canny ability to make a profit even while enemies were calling for her arrest showed that she was a woman to be reckoned with. No one guessed it then, least of all Mme. Restell herself, but she would follow her trade with surprising success, with but one setback in nearly four decades, on the way to becoming the most notorious of her kind in the city.

The character of the town itself went a long way toward making her success assured. It was a robust, bawdy, roistering town that had sent thousands around the Horn to the California gold rush of '49 without losing its own atmosphere of a get-rich-quick community, hiding its feet of clay under a cloak of respectability. There were churches by the score but there were saloons, brothels, gambling dens, and dance halls where life was cheap and morals even cheaper.

New York had weathered the Astor Place riots fought over the relative merits of two Shakespearean actors—one American and one English. It had welcomed Jenny

Lind to its communal bosom as P. T. Barnum grew rich on the songbird's power to mesmerize her listeners. It had marveled at its first true multimillionaire, John Jacob Astor, who had trapped and bartered for furs in the wilds of the Pacific northwest and invested the money in Manhattan real estate, which seemed to have no way to go in value but up. He had died, legend had it, a wreck of a man, so broken in health he could eat only mother's milk drawn from the breasts of wet nurses; but he had amassed a fabulous fortune, established a fantastic family, and given momentum to a gold-encrusted society.

The residential district had moved steadily uptown, first from below Chambers Street, then along Broadway as far as Broome Street, at which point various conservatives said it had gone as far as it should. But Washington Square beckoned and then Fifth Avenue and Broadway, clear to Madison Square. The city fathers did their best to get the town out of the mud, contracting with various entrepreneurs to pave the main avenues with Belgian blocks or other lasting materials. It was all a woman could do to cross the street without getting the hem of her skirt soaked with muddy water. Everyone who was anyone had a horse and carriage, which led to such a cluttering of the streets that each afternoon was a nightmare of dashing steeds, whirling wheels, drivers with writhing whips, and drays loaded with huge quantities of whatever a growing community might need.

This was the New York the casual visitor saw—all turmoil, expansion, and excitement. The other side was not as attractive. The waterfronts on both rivers were commercial areas by day and eyesores by night. Once the cargo from the many ships had been unloaded and safely stored in warehouses and the sun had gone down, Front, Water, South, and Washington Streets took on another aspect. Saloons opened, pool halls became busy, and the brothels did a thriving business. A man who ventured at night into these streets had to be brave or careless. Edward Dicey, a reporter for the *London Spectator*, visited the metropolis during the early months of the Civil War and described it for his English readers:

"For an Anglo-Saxon population, there is little drunkenness visible in the streets; and with regard to other forms of public vice it is not for an Englishman to speak severely. The Broadway saloons, with their so-called 'pretty waiter-girls,' and the Lager Bier haunts in the low quarters of town, whose windows are crowded with wretched half-dressed, or undressed women, form indeed, about the most shameless exhibition of public vice I have ever come across, even in England or Holland."

It must have sounded glamorous in Victorian England —and very naughty—but these sinful pleasures were well out of reach of the bulk of the residents. These unfortunates lived in squalid hovels, rickety warrens and shanties where running water was unknown, sewers equally unheard of; where fire was an enemy that annually took a grisly toll of children and the elderly.

Five Points, that neighborhood between the Bowery and the present Civic Center, was one vast hellhole. It was a slum where crime was the way of life and poverty chained the decent to an existence unfit for animals.

One building, known as the Old Brewery, had once been just that, but then it was transformed into a dwelling place fronting on an opening called Paradise Square, near present-day Chinatown. The inhabitants covered the spectrum from decent but destitute families to prostitutes, gamblers, dope addicts, and quite a few Chinese opium smokers. It was too decrepit to renovate and too evil to endure, so the Ladies' Home Missionary Society bought it, in order, the papers said, that it be replaced and "changed from a pest-house of sin into a school of virtue."

It was not the only place of its kind by any means. The Children's Aid Society asked the public for funds to put a training school at the foot of East 42nd Street, at the East River, next to the slum called Dutch Hill. The monumental buildings of the United Nations are located there now. This may have been the worst section in all New York. As an observer described it:

"The houses are little more than board and mud shanties, scattered around like the wigwams of an Indian village. Some are primitive, with a hole in the roof for the smoke to emerge, or a railroad car banked as a house. When the owners move they sell their shanties for $5 or $10."

Most of the inhabitants were Irish and German laborers and their families, so poor that hardened criminals avoided the place, knowing there was nothing of profit to steal. The women and children tried to add to the family income by selling rags and bones collected in the better sections of the city.

By one of those flukes that make social history so intriguing, the hovels of Dutch Hill counted as one of their closest neighbors the old Beekman mansion, once the "country home" of the famous family that played a vital role in the Revolutionary War and the establishment of New York State. This house had been the scene of socially elegant soirées and political gatherings, and had also harbored two famous men—if only for one night each.

Major John André, who conspired to obtain the secrets of West Point's fortifications and the other defenses of the mid-Hudson Valley, slept at the Beekman House on the night before he journeyed upriver to meet the traitor

Benedict Arnold. It was in this house, too, that the British kept Captain Nathan Hale on the night before he was hanged as a spy. By the time the immigrants from Germany and Ireland had settled at Dutch Hill, forlorn at not finding gold in the streets of the new world, the Beekman mansion was a down-at-the-heels reminder of the opulence of an earlier generation.

New York was surely a city of paradoxes. Cattle from the west were still driven to the New Jersey bank of the Hudson, transported from Bull's Ferry there to Manhattanville in New York, and then down the west side of Manhattan to the slaughterhouses. The same year that the ferry opened—it was 1850—James Fenimore Cooper, the novelist, wrote to his wife that a Mrs. Wetmore wore a new party dress costing $30,000. Even the amateur investor will realize that at that time in the city's development, $30,000 would have bought a sizable interest in a tramcar railway, a department store, or an express company. Three years later the Dr. Townsend who had compounded sarsaparilla syrup, a great favorite in the candy kitchens, built a house on the corner of 34th Street and Fifth Avenue which cost, with the property, $200,000.

If you were staying at the Astor House on lower Broadway you would not know about the Old Brewery at Five Points or Dutch Hill; but as one writer said, if you looked out the front across at P. T. Barnum's Museum something of the backward conditions would be evident. There were "barrels, baskets, decayed tea chests, earthenware crocks and boxes all over the sidewalks, all filled with coal ashes."

About this time the famous English novelist William Makepeace Thackeray visited the United States on a lecture tour. It was eminently successful. Americans, even those on the edge of a frontier existence, hungered for culture and Thackeray spoke to capacity audiences every-

24

where. When he sailed on the Cunarder *Europa* it was with real regret on his part. He had fallen in love with the big, brash, sprawling metropolis. A few nights out at sea he attended a gala ship's party and he delighted in showing several passengers his watch, still set at New York time, although the ship's clock had been set ahead several times. He described the scene in this odd way: "I said, There, that's the real time—they said: Isn't this a beautiful ball and says I—Pish—this is nothing—go to New York if you want to see what a ball is—as if there could be any balls after New York."

This, then, was the city where Mary Applegate was delivered of her baby and where Mme. Restell was already growing disenchanted with the run-down neighborhood on Greenwich Street where she maintained her office. Some months later Mayor Fernando Wood urged his aldermen to vote for a new courthouse somewhere on Madison Square on the grounds that "Chambers Street is too far downtown." The lady physician did not agree with the chief magistrate of the city, and as if to prove her independence, she moved out of the little frame house down near the river and into much more spacious quarters on the aforementioned Chambers Street. Now within only a few steps of City Hall, she felt that she had "arrived."

ALL BUSINESSMEN
WERE PROSPERING

When fashionable women paid fees of several hundred dollars to Mme. Restell for an abortion, the financial pain was assuaged by the knowledge that money was easy to come by, was not taxed, and could be invested at incredibly high interest rates if the owner was willing to take risks. It was an era of sudden boom—with a few busts, of course—when men of vision could make a fortune by providing a needed service for the growing population of New York.

Cornelius Vanderbilt began his business career as a deckhand on the ferryboats shuttling between Staten Island and Manhattan. In a few years he had purchased several steamers and was offering steamboat service up the Hudson River and along Long Island Sound to the busy ports of New England. The gold rush to California electrified him, not with dreams of gold nuggets washed from mountain streams, but with fantasies of increased business for his steam vessels. He quickly instituted a service running out of New York and down to the Isthmus of Panama, where passengers went overland through

Nicaragua to the Pacific for transfer to other ships that carried them to California. It was smart thinking for a ferryboat man. Four years after the first gold strike at Sutter's Mill, the "Commodore," as he preferred to be called, confided to his cronies that he was worth a cool $11 million earning interest at 25 percent.

Jenny Lind made $12,600 for her first appearance at Castle Garden in Battery Place and old Phineas Barnum pocketed something in the neighborhood of $300,000 for the entire tour of "the Swedish Nightingale." James Gordon Bennett was doing well with the two-penny paper he had founded and the railroad boom was creating millionaires.

With all this money being accumulated, Mme. Restell could count on a steady income. Even those clients who were not well-to-do could usually force the men responsible for getting them into a "delicate condition" to find the money that would keep the scandal quiet.

Although she probably never met him, the *Herald*'s publisher—swaggering, conceited, and fearless Jim Bennett—was of great assistance to the midwife and abortionist. He was the first publisher in the city to realize that there were more poor people than wealthy, and that he could build a readership more quickly by siding with the poor. So he quarreled with the vested interests, criticized the self-righteous, and ran almost any advertisement offered for his columns. It was Bennett who ordered his reporters and writers to stop using the word *limbs* and substitute the word *legs*. Eyebrows went up when he boldly printed words like *shirts* for *linens* and *pantaloons* for *unmentionables*. When he tangled with the clergy, they declared a holy war against him but it only sent his circulation figures higher.

Bennett fell in love with a pretty young Irish woman,

Henrietta Crean, and announced his intention to marry her in his paper under a headline that was explicit, if not, by modern standards, well-balanced. It bore this message:

TO THE READERS OF THE HERALD——DECLARATION OF
LOVE——CAUGHT AT LAST——GOING TO BE MARRIED——
NEW MOVEMENT IN CIVILIZATION

The story went on to say Henrietta possessed a fortune: her purity and uprightness being worth a half million, her good sense and elegance another half million, and such attributes as soul, mind, and beauty easily valued "at millions on millions."

After the wedding ceremony Bennett and his bride went for a honeymoon to Niagara Falls and all went well until he returned to the city. He wanted to stay at the Astor House until their new home was completed, but his enemies influenced the hotel manager to refuse them a room. Bennett called them blockheads in his paper and pursued his brash way. William Cullen Bryant, editor of the *Evening Post*, would not even speak to him, and his other rivals excoriated him as a sensation monger, but Bennett's paper went on selling.

It is possible that without a lusty paper like the *Herald* printing scandalous stories and carrying highly unethical advertising Mme. Restell would have been unable to stay in business. Before Bennett's paper broke open the crust of propriety and false righteousness, the journals had contented themselves with long discourses on morality, boring accounts of European politics, and excerpts from staid, semireligious tracts and books. The *Herald* opened the people's eyes to the newsworthiness of their town, and titillating gossip became a highly salable product.

Another factor playing into the abortionist's hands was the existence of hundreds of fashionable boarding houses. Frances Trollope, mother of the great English novelist, was amazed by the multitude of such places. "A great number of young married persons board by the year instead of going to housekeeping," she wrote to friends at home, and then expatiated on this theme in her book on American manners and customs. She noted, as did others, that the wealthier couples took suites at the Astor House from which they journeyed in summer to mansions on the Hudson or Long Island.

Block after block of these boarding houses and residential hotels were supported by families who could not afford the high rents then current or could not find servants to their liking. Another English observer was even more blunt than Mrs. Trollope, assigning as the chief reason for the existence of so many boarding houses "the indisposition of young ladies to undertake the responsibilities and troubles of attending to domestic arrangements."

If these boarding houses provided a sort of false front for the homemakers, it was nothing to the false fronts afforded women by the fashions of the post–Civil War era. Talk about fraud and deceit! Stores like A. T. Stewart's emporium on Broadway between Chambers and Reade Streets, Bogert and Mecamley's on Ninth Avenue, and Cochran, McLean, and Company did a thriving business in "glorifying" female figures. As one social historian describes it:

"It was the age of symmetry and modesty. Women exhibited the exact antithesis of the boyish form. We liked our girls with plenty of meat on them in those days. The ideal figure was a waspish 18-inch waist, the high voluptuous palpitating thirty-six bust, and a pair of wide and aggressive hips. If Nature did not provide them, the kindly art of man supplied the deficiency. Numerous bust forms of padded cotton, inflated rubber and woven wire netting met with a ready sale. Sometimes, during a 'spooning party,' as it was called in those days, the rubber kind would collapse with a muffled bang, to the consternation of the wearer and to the hilarious merriment of the party of the second part." To attain what this writer had termed "aggressive hips," the ladies turned to bustles, which gave extraordinary dimensions to that portion of their anatomy. Circumspect designers referred to this area as "the Grecian Bend."

In view of this particular preformation of feminine contours, it was hardly strange that Jenny Lind stirred varying reactions among those who saw her for the first time. Barnum told the lawyer who had drawn up the financial contract for the singer's tour that he was about to introduce him to a most remarkable person. Not knowing the attorney had already caught a glimpse of the diva, the impresario said, "I'm going to introduce you to an angel, sir—to an angel." The lawyer accepted the offer, muttering under his breath that "she looked wonderfully substantial for an angel."

In a way, New York was like the ladies—all padded to appear more attractive than it really was. The fine buildings on Broadway hid the wretched warrens of the side streets. Cholera and smallpox and typhoid fever took hideous tolls each time an epidemic swept over the city, but deaths among children from diarrhea, spread by flies from horse droppings in the streets—though much less spectacular—far outnumbered the others.

Immigrants by the thousands were dumped at the piers as Europe sent its poor to the new world in search of a better life. Some found employment upstate digging the Erie Canal, some took up farm land then selling for ridiculously low prices, but most of them, lacking funds to travel farther, settled in the seaport city. For every Mrs. Wetmore with her $30,000 ball gown, there were thousands of women with no more clothes than those on their backs. For every music lover who paid $30 to hear Miss Lind sing there were thousands of men whose daily income was measured in pennies.

It was primarily to the upper strata of society that Mme. Restell sold her infallible French pills and for whom she performed abortions. She knew where the money was. Yet she also aborted women and delivered some unwanted children for women who had very little of the world's goods.

She never gave her reasons. It could have been mere greed that motivated her to take every dollar in sight and enrich herself. But a psychiatrist trying to recreate her character might ask if she had not been led to serve the poor out of a sense of fairness. A woman in her position could easily have reflected that there was no justice when rich women could afford to hide their sins while poor women could not. And she could have thought back to her earlier days when poverty beset her both in England and during her first years in the new land. The fact remains that Mme. Restell did care for many poor women and it is ironic that the first person who caused her trouble with the law was one of those at the very bottom of the social ladder—a rustic widower's housemaid.

A GIRL FROM THE
COUNTRY

Maria Bodine was born and grew up in the small village
of Montgomery, N.Y., not far from Newburgh. In her
late teens her family moved to Ramapo, a hamlet just
north of the New Jersey border and about twenty miles
in from the Hudson River. She was of average size, not
particularly attractive, and without self-assurance.

As she was uneducated, there was little for her to do
except work as a domestic servant, earning a few dollars
a week and her room and board. Although she figured in
one of the longest trials held in the East up to the time
of the Civil War, not much is known about her childhood.
But it became apparent at the trial that she, like many
other girls in the same position, became a prey to the men
in whose homes she worked.

It appeared, on the basis of testimony in the court, that
she had no strong antipathy for sex out of wedlock; it
was even insinuated that she was inordinately fond of it.
At any rate, she went to work for Joseph P. Cook, a
farmer who operated a small cotton mill on the side in
Walden, N.Y. Cook was a widower with a son of ten and

a daughter of nine. Before the first month was out Maria and Cook had found mutual interests so strong that the widower was spending most of his evenings in Maria's bedroom. By May 1846 she realized that she was pregnant and turned to the mill owner for aid. Maria was then about twenty-five years old.

Cook was in no position to have his behavior exposed in a small Orange County town, so he sent Maria to Mme. Restell in New York, knowing that the big city was the safest place to hide unwelcome facts—or that it had that reputation. Unknown to both of them, Mme. Restell's establishment had been staked out by the authorities who were finally seeking evidence against the abortionist. Maria was followed from the house on Greenwich Street, questioned by assistant district attorneys, and persuaded to sign a complaint.

This was the background of what became known as the "Wonderful trial of Anna Caroline Lohman, alias Restell," a trial that lasted eighteen days and set the city agog with excitement. Men crowded the halls of the Court of General Sessions and fought for seats in the courtroom. Women may have also wished to attend, but to confess such an interest publicly would have been unthinkable; they stayed away, waiting for secondhand news.

Rumors had been all that most people could feed on during the early days of Mme. Restell's activities, so the open trial promised to be a sensation and to reveal just how depraved the woman was. At least half of the population had very strong opinions about the whole matter. The trial would expose the abortionist's activities and, it was hoped, support their own beliefs. Gossip is rich fare at any table; when it is supported by hard facts it is especially tasty.

The trial opened on October 25, 1847. The time was

ripe for such a newsworthy event. The War of 1812 was forgotten by all except the old and the Civil War had not yet loomed on the horizon. The California gold rush itself was two years away. There seemed to be a news vacuum, which Mme. Restell's trial now filled.

The accused woman was charged on five counts of manslaughter, four of them alleging that she committed abortion upon the body of Maria Bodine while pregnant with a quick child (one that had already given signs of life) and one of abortion involving a child not quick. District Attorney McKeon was leaving nothing to chance. If convicted on one of the first counts the female "physician" could face a four-year term in prison; if convicted only on the fifth count, the penalty would be a one-year term in the penitentiary.

This was well before the era of photojournalism, and all we have to inform us what the scene was like, other than the printed word, is a drawing of Mme. Restell made on the opening day by an artist of the *National Police Gazette*. The accused is shown, head and shoulders, with a bonnet tied under her chin—and a most formidable chin it was. Her eyes are wide-set and her nose straight and regular, but it is her lips that seem to reveal her character. They are set in a straight, severe line, absolutely devoid of warmth or softness. It is as if they were the jaws of a small vise, screwed tight together and unlikely to open easily. This impression was noted in the press, although it must be said that few prisoners show a humorous or relaxed face at their trial.

Anna was attended by her husband, the printer from the *Herald*, and reporters remarked that she had no female companion and that no other person of her sex was present in the packed courtroom.

Assistant District Attorney Jonas B. Phillips sat with

A courtroom artist's impression of Madame Restell, drawn for the
National Police Gazette *on the opening day of her trial,*
October 25, 1847.

the chief prosecutor, and so did Ogden Hoffman, brought into the case to aid in the prosecution. Mme. Restell was defended by two of the best criminal lawyers in the city, James T. Brady and David Graham. Judge Scott presided in a room that one newspaper said was "crowded to suffocation."

Picking a jury proved most troublesome. Very few men—there were no women on juries then—could say with honesty that they had formed no opinion. The Restell case was the talk of the town, and either each venireman had actually decided on the defendant's guilt or innocence or was a little ashamed to say publicly that he knew so little about the notorious issue at law that he had come to no conclusions.

After the first prospective jurors had been excused, Richard Venables, a hosiery merchant of Canal Street, was accepted by both prosecution and defense and was named juror-in-chief, as the title went in those days. All day long the process continued, but when the session ended only three men sat in the jury box.

The next day was not much better. A grocer, J. B. Anderson, of Horatio Street, was accepted when he said he had seen no words or sketches to lead him to an opinion. What he had read had made no impression and he had no unfavorable notions at all. This persuaded both sides that he was an ideal juror and he was accepted.

Another talesman, a bootmaker, had his mind made up. The district attorney was suspicious.

"Do you know what the prisoner is indicted for?" he asked.

"Yes," replied the bootmaker, "for bigamy."

This inability to differentiate between bigamy and the present charge caused him to be excused. When evening came there were only three more men in the box, although more than two panels of 100 names each had been exhausted. The jury was completed on the third day, but everyone was exhausted and court was adjourned.

Early the next morning the assistant district attorney got down to business, or at least to business as it was then handled in American courtrooms. "The holiest spot in the Temple of Justice," he said, "is the jury box; sympathy, prejudice or passion cannot enter it; ye are then withdrawn from the world and all its external influences, the stern, honest and inflexible ministers of justice, whose decision the guilty alone await with terror and apprehension, but to whom innocence ever looks with confidence and never-dying hope."

Phillips then read from the Act of July 1846 under which the charges were brought and went on:

> The heart sickens at such a narrative. Nature is appalled that woman, the last and loveliest of her works, could so unsex herself as to perpetrate such fiend-like enormities. The gardener watches, with jealous care, the seed he casts into the fertile earth, until it germs, and buds, and blooms. But this defendant destroys the germ of nature—she kills the unborn infant; endangers, if she does not destroy, the mother's life, ruins her health; and all for the sake of the base lucre, which she allures the frail, or wicked, who have fallen, to pay her, in the vain hope that she can aid them to conceal their shame.

Thousands of other words, just as flowery, were cast before the jurors to impress them with the seriousness of the case. Then he called the first witness, Maria Bodine.

The complainant entered the room with what was described as "a feeble, tottering walk." One reporter said she was "evidently in a rapid decline of health." In a voice but little above a whisper, Maria said she had had intercourse with Cook within a month of her being hired but that it was some considerable time before she became aware that she was "in the family way." There must have ensued acrimonious conversations between the housemaid and the widower, because it was several months before she won him over to the need for drastic action. Then, she testified, she took the Erie railroad from Ramapo to Piermont, on the Hudson, and the boat down to the city. It was midnight when she arrived in Manhattan, so slow were the trains and so long the wait in Piermont. Maria stayed several days with a sister on Bleecker Street before visiting Mme. Restell's.

"How did you discover the house?" she was asked.

"I saw the number in the newspapers," said Maria, showing the value of advertising.

Mme. Restell, the witness testified, told her an examination would cost $5 and an operation, $100. She also said she had pills at $1 and others at $5 that would "bring me right," but that she would prefer the young woman to board with her at $5 a week until she was delivered naturally of her baby. Maria said she told the defendant she would have preferred to do that but "my beau would object to the charge." The witness said she left the house, was followed by an officer and her name taken.

Under questioning by the assistant district attorney, Maria, blushing and hesitant, was forced to tell in the courtroom crowded with curious men how she came to know she was pregnant, how she felt, and the last bitter detail of her decision to seek out the ladies' physician for help. Nothing that was written by the reporters for the press nor by the pamphleteers who rushed their versions into print as fast as they could after the trial mentioned the outrage of Maria's exploitation. None remarked that women should have the same right as men to decide whether they wanted to become parents. Under the laws as they then existed Maria was a chattel. She had sinned and had to pay for it in public.

After her first conversation with Mme. Restell, the witness said, she returned to Ramapo where she stayed a fortnight before coming again to the city. She did not discuss the delay, but it was evident that her "beau" had at first hesitated to finance an illegal operation but had finally consented. He sent one of his cotton weavers, John McCann, with the housemaid and $30, which did not satisfy Mme. Restell.

Alternately weeping and simpering, Maria told how she had stayed at the house on Greenwich Street while McCann and the "physician" haggled over the fee. Mme. Restell finally agreed to a cut rate and McCann went back to Ramapo to get the balance of the money from Cook. It was on a Sunday, Maria recalled, that McCann gave the rest of the fee to Mme. Restell, and within a few hours the abortionist performed the operation.

No one else was present. There was neither nurse, attendant, nor any other person to assist if things went wrong. The jurors sat on the edges of their chairs. Step by step, Maria told of the agony caused by such an operation performed without anesthesia, how she groaned and cried out. Mme. Restell gave her pills to bring on the desired delivery—and to cut down the pain, the witness said.

Monday, she told the jury, was a day of horror. She felt worse and worse and kept crying out in pain. "Monday night," added Maria, "Mme. Restell slept with me. I was in great agony all the night."

There followed many examinations, all painful beyond

belief, and she took more pills. She lost track of the passage of time, but about a day or two later, she thought, she had the induced miscarriage brought on by the operation and the "infallible" pills.

"She hurt me so," continued the girl, cowering in the witness chair, "that I halloed out and gripped hold of her hand; she told me to have patience, and I would call her 'mother' for it. She did not say anything at that time more particular in reference to my pain; when I again told her, she said my pains were after-pains."

By Thursday afternoon, Maria said, she wanted to leave the Restell house. "I had crackers and tea, the first day," she said, "then afterwards some vegetables and soup. On Thursday afternoon she came into the room and found me crying; and she asked me what was the matter. I told her I wanted to go home, but I had no money to go with. If I wished to go, she said, she would give me money to pay my passage and get some refreshments. She gave me a dollar. My passage money was six shillings. (A shilling, still in use in the United States, was worth $12\frac{1}{2}$ cents.) She then took me down into the parlor and gave me some wine. She said she would listen and look around to see if any officers were about.

"She looked out and said there were not. She said if anyone arrested or accosted me, I must return to her, and I should go in a carriage. She said I must say nothing to anyone about what had been done; if I told, she said we should both be liable to the State's prison, as I had no right to go there, and she had no right to give me medicine, *or to do it.* My breasts pained me very much, and milk came from them over my dress. On telling her, she said if they troubled me very much, I must wrap them in red flannel and rub them with camphor."

Maria left the Restell establishment, she told the jury,

about three or four in the afternoon. "She shook hands with me on parting, gave me a kiss, and told me I must never do so again. I then left."

Her testimony about her days of agony had drained all her strength, it seemed to reporters in the courtroom, but the session went on while she told of her painful trip back to Walden, where she stayed at a sister's house. The sister, Mrs. Beriah Youngblood, was a widow of a month or so and was so frightened by the young woman's appearance that she summoned a Dr. Edwin Evans to care for her. In the course of the next two months or so Dr. Evans called in five other physicians at different times.

At this point, Judge Scott took mercy on the witness and adjourned court for the day, but not until the prosecutors had brought out one further bit of testimony. "Maria," asked Phillips, "what is the present condition of your health?"

"My health is still feeble; I have constant distress in my head; pains, falling of the womb; weakness in my back, burning in my hands, weakness and trembling all over me."

A newspaperman, touched by the woman's demeanor, told his readers: "The witness, pale and agitated, was assisted by an officer from the stand, and left it with feeble and faltering steps, evidently laboring under severe pains about the spine and loins." If he had been a physician he could not have been more accurate in describing how a woman who had subjected herself to an abortion under such primitive conditions would have felt after so brutal an experience.

The next day—the fifth—Maria was cross-examined by Brady. "The witness must put aside her veil and turn to the jury," he ordered, "so that her answers may be heard. My cross-examination will be long and severe, and if at any time she be exhausted, I will pay every attention to her state, much as I have been used to these faintings." Brady indicated he would be fair, but that he did not trust the witness's histrionics. Apparently, the defense counsel was out for an acquittal, and would let no considerate feelings interfere. Almost at once he won an admission that the witness had had intercourse with Cook at least once a week for about two years. "Had you ever had intercourse with any other person before you had with Mr. Cook?" asked the attorney.

"This is one of those questions which the witness may or may not answer," interjected the district attorney. "But, I advise her to answer."

The question was repeated but Maria Bodine declined to reply.

"This woman had for years, constantly and habitually, indulged in prostitution," shouted Brady, "and she *shall* answer."

Judge Scott interposed that he was bound to protect the witness if she preferred to remain silent.

"No mawkish sensibility here," said Brady. "This woman is guilty. We have no sympathy for her, but shall use her as we think proper. She is the felon, the instigator, the prompter. The defendant had requested her to wait her time. She would not. I shall show that the pretense that Mr. Cook *ever* had intercourse with her is false and abominable. She never was pregnant. She had for years been accustomed to have free promiscuous intercourse with men. That witness is guilty as much as the accused, and ought as much to be tried."

"I don't pretend to have a virgin upon the stand coming from Restell's house," retorted the district attorney. "It is an impossibility and we do not pretend that she is a woman of immaculate character."

Graham then entered the debate and argued that Maria's delicate health resulted from causes other than abortion.

"It is caused by a long course of intemperance, a constant career of prostitution, and is the natural consequence—not of Madame Restell, but of habitual and promiscuous intercourse as a harlot—not with Mr. Cook, but with every man, every hour, or every five minutes of her life," said Graham.

Maria collapsed and had to be helped from the stand to recuperate in an anteroom. When she returned Brady tore into her story again, asking her if she had ever had a venereal disease. There was more legal argument, the court ruling that she did not have to answer if she wished not to. The witness declined on the ground that the question "tended to degrade her."

She went over the story of her first visit to the Restell house and told of being followed by an officer.

"I don't know the name of the officer who followed me," she said. "He was within a few doors on the other side of the street when I came out. He went all the way home with me to my sister's. He told me that I had been in a bad murderer's house, and it was his orders to take me home for the purpose of taking my name and residence. He asked me if I had purchased any medicine, and I said I had not.

"I told him I was very unwell and I went to consult her as a female physician. He did not ask me and I did not tell him what was the matter with me."

The morning of the next court day Maria went back to the stand to tell of her difficulties when she reached home after the operation. Dr. Evans treated her, she said.

"I think he gave me powders," said the witness. "I took to my bed. He cupped me on the back, he leeched me to my bowels, he put issues in my back." (All of these steps involved drawing blood from the patient: by an incision allowing blood to run into a cup, by letting leeches suck it out of the tissues, and by using different chemicals.)

During an unusual evening session on the sixth day of the trial Maria discussed her appearance before the grand jury at the state's expense while waiting to testify. She was then excused, much to her relief.

Dr. Samuel C. Smith, a physician practicing in Montgomery, was the next to take the stand, saying he had also acted as Overseer of the Poor and had been called in to care for the complainant. "I called at Youngblood's to grant temporary relief as an overseer," he testified. "She was enabled to be removed to the Alms-house on the 8th of May. She required medical aid; she was in a very delicate condition."

After an examination on the fifth of June he was sure of the cause of her illness. "As a medical man I considered the cause of her illness, from my examination, to be either that she must have had a delivery of a child badly managed, or must have had an abortion produced upon her, or by some mechanical injury by an instrument, or by violence of the hand," he said.

Later it was brought out by the prosecutor that it was this same Dr. Smith who initiated the investigation leading to Mme. Restell's arrest. The physician said he wrote to the Mayor of New York City on August 2 and that four days later a police officer appeared to question Maria Bodine. She was subsequently taken to New York by the district attorney's men.

The chief defense counsel sought to elicit information concerning a rumored statement that Dr. Smith was said to have made about the Restell case.

"Have you said to anyone what purpose you had in

view [in writing to the Mayor]?" asked Brady. "Do you know a George Millspaw?"

"I know George Millspaw," rejoined the doctor on the stand. "I think I did not tell him I would make a good thing out of this prosecution before I got through." Some of his neighbors had whispered to outsiders that Dr. Smith hoped to profit by the case.

And there the matter stood during a long exchange over whether Maria's symptoms could have arisen from causes other than an abortion, particularly from interrupted menstruation.

Dr. Evans was called to the stand to tell of his visits to Maria after her return home. He repeated the by now familiar description of the young woman's ill health and told of what he did to make her well, and of a ruse he used to protect her.

"I never told anyone of her disease," he said, "till some months after I had ceased attending her. While I attended her nobody but myself knew, but as a ruse, and to divert people's attention; I said she had a disease in her spine, to conceal her shame. I ceased to attend her because I had a considerable bill against them, and they had no means of paying, and having done my share I thought the town of Montgomery might do the rest."

To counter the defense contention that Maria was not pregnant when she visited Mme. Restell's, the district attorney called on a number of physicians who treated the woman. All said that every indication pointed to the fact that she had been pregnant shortly before they examined her. Additional evidence to this effect came from Ellen Call, a neighbor of Mr. Cook's.

"Did you notice any peculiarity about her in July of 1846?" asked the prosecutor.

"Yes," replied Miss Call, "she had her head tied up

and she had to have her clothes open, unhooked, as they had grown very tight. . . ."

"When did you again see her?"

"The next time I saw her was in about a week or ten days after that."

"How did she look then?"

"She looked just like a person risen from the grave."

For several days witnesses gave technical testimony concerning the signs of pregnancy, when quickening of the unborn fetus is first noticed, and other symptoms. Much of this testimony dealt with the appearance of a pregnant woman's breasts, particularly the dark coloring called the areola that came at the base of the nipples. This subject intrigued the jurors and for the first time in the trial they insisted on a full description. The defense attorney objected that the matter had been fully covered, but the court overruled him.

"When the jury do not perhaps understand a subject, or a question," he said, "they are entitled to ask for any additional information, and they must have it."

"The majority of us wish for it," said several jurors. So Dr. Evans gave a full answer.

"The appearance around the nipple, called the areola, is quite dark, deep brown, a kind of circle, broad around the edge," he explained. "It was distinctly marked in Maria Bodine. . . . I examined particularly that I might not criminate her falsely. She was using flannel saturated with vinegar, applied to the bosom."

The jurors now seemed satisfied and the state called in other medical men to support its case. The very first found himself questioned about the previous matter.

"Is the areola considered by standard writers [of textbooks] an evidence of pregnancy?" Dr. Gunning Bedford was asked. Dr. Bedford cited a singular anecdote described by one medical author. "This physician, Dr. Hunter, was dissecting the corpse of a young woman who had died in a city hospital and found the young lady's bosom was marked by a distinctive areola; he asserted that she had been or was then pregnant, though during life she was regarded strictly as a virgin, and also the membrane, called the hymen, was not ruptured. Dr. Hunter's diagnosis on this most improbable case turned out perfectly correct, as the young female on examination proved to be *enceinte*, and a child existed."

Mr. Hoffman, taking over the examination, asked Dr. Bedford for medical information concerning the commoner techniques for inducing an abortion. The witness said the hand or an instrument was ordinarily used.

"Suppose the hand were introduced and worked 'round and 'round, as has been described, what would be the effects?" he was asked.

"The most horrible," replied Dr. Bedford.

"Could a wire be under the finger at the time of such an operation?"

"Undoubtedly; that's the way the thing is done."

The next morning's newspapers carried their reporters' comments, along with the transcript, and in one journal this part of the testimony was followed by the phrase: (Great sensation throughout the court!)

More testimony followed, most of it to substantiate earlier witnesses, and at the end of the eighth day the state rested.

"GO,
AND SIN NO MORE"

The next morning the chief counsel for Mme. Restell opened his case with a burst of oratory.

"I feel entire confidence, Gentlemen, in your integrity," he said. "I repose a full reliance on your pure, and honorable and upright minds, and whatever your decision be, though there can be but one decision, but whether my client, the prisoner before you, by some inconceivable misfortune be found guilty of the offense alleged in this most singular and irregular indictment, or she walk forth out of this hall, as she ought to do, innocent, perfectly innocent, with repute unstained, and character unblemished —I shall bow with due respect, and full submission to the mature opinion of twelve upright and enlightened jurors."

Brady digressed to excoriate the editors of the *Sun*, who had that very morning, according to the fiery defense attorney, come out editorially for a conviction.

"The article," he said, "tried to ensure the conviction of the prisoner, whether right or wrong, and by the most industrious of efforts, endeavors to destroy her at all hazards—and if she cannot be found guilty of murder, like a Yorkshire jury, to convict her of horse stealing."

Emulating many another attorney before and since, he protested against the conduct of the "low portion of the press," then went back to the subject of the state's behavior. "I have seen females brought out of that green room, as it were, or rehearsal chamber, veiled and modestly attired . . . and denunciations have been heaped and piled up against us by certain of the press, yet the jurors swerved not from their duty." Brady's voice rose and fell like an English actor declaiming Shakespeare.

"But counsel did not quail," he continued, "and *that very female*, elaborately trimmed up for a witness as she was, turned out the veriest harlot, the foulest trull that infests our streets or emerges from the purlieus of the [Five] Points,—she proved a thief, a vagrant, and the lowest prostitute who draggles her dank wet skirts through the mud, and offers her loathsome person for hire, to the cheapest bidder!"

The mayor did not escape the fire of Mr. Brady's attack; he was accused of intervening out of "zeal" to convict Mme. Restell. But it was Maria Bodine who earned his greatest contempt: "This woman, this prosecutrix, it will be our solemn duty to prove, and we have facts to sustain us in the assertion that that woman is as foul, corrupt, loathsome, guilty a thing, as ever polluted God's blessed earth by her pestilential presence."

Brady also attacked the district attorney for insinuating that his client had been niggardly in giving Maria so little money when she left the house on Greenwich Street. "Madame Restell gave her a parting kiss, and the salutary counsel, 'Go, and sin no more,' " said the defense attorney. "But then she gave her only six shillings for her passage by the cars, and only two shillings for refreshments on the road. Only two shillings for refreshments on a journey of about 60 miles, occupying, it may be, only three hours. Only two shillings for so distant a journey. Why I have seen old matrons, nice country-women, go to Bridgeport, 60 miles, with only two cents worth of doughnuts in their pocket, and three cents of ginger cake in their reticule; they have never thought of any thing more; and I myself have traveled through that country; and so little was the demand for luxuries on the road that I have seen a pile of oysters which had died from consumption, and perished from want of excitement."

Mr. Brady's opening statement included other charges against the state's witnesses, particularly Dr. Smith, who had enlisted the interest of the Mayor of New York in the Bodine case, and John McCann, Maria's companion on her trips from Ramapo to New York. When this was done, Brady made one more appeal to the jury to act in fairness—an appeal that stirred the courtroom, newsmen said, as courtrooms had seldom been stirred before.

"I solemnly adjure you, gentlemen, to do your duty to your country and to my client, the prisoner now before you, strictly, firmly, and impartially, as I have endeavoured to discharge mine. And if there be any truth in that sacred prayer which we all address to Almighty God, in our last parting hour; if there be any truth in the forms of earthly justice, the overwhelming conviction on my mind is, and I most solemnly believe, that my client must be acquitted by your verdict."

Without an instant's respite from his ardent defense of Mme. Restell, Brady started calling witnesses to prove that Maria Bodine's character was no model for nice girls. Mrs. Deborah Tiers, a neighbor in Walden, could find little good to say about the chief witness for the state. She said she had heard Maria say she was "in the family way" so often she did not believe it when she heard it after the girl's stay at the Cook house, and she also asserted that Maria had claimed to be pregnant by the bartender in a local tavern. This was several years before her going to Cook as a housekeeper.

A goodly number of ladies in Walden apparently were much affected by Maria's condition just before her visit to Mme. Restell's and after her return home. Mrs. Tiers said there was considerable gossip. "Mrs. Hatch, Mrs. Dowling and I thought it very strange, to us," she testified. "We consulted together, we talked, we did not know what *ailded* her." Mrs. Tiers added that she had often talked with Maria about her conduct. "The doctor was attending her," the witness said. "She had formerly told me herself that it was the case that she was pregnant by Morris Vernoy and I told her she had better get married."

On the tenth day of the trial Maria fared very badly. The aforementioned friends of Mrs. Tiers, Mrs. Catherine Dowling and Mrs. Chrissy Jane Hatch, both told the jurors that "it was the voice of the people, the general talk of one and all, that she was a bad character." Mrs. Hatch, the mother of nine children, revealed how the Bodine woman's behavior had disrupted the normal course of rustic life in Walden. It should have been apparent to everyone in the courtroom that this Walden in Orange County shared none of the peace and quiet Thoreau described when writing of another Walden farther north. "I one day happened to say to Mrs. Youngblood that her sister Maria was *grunting* a little too much," said Mrs. Hatch. "Mrs. Youngblood said that if Mrs. Tiers and myself did not hold our tongues she would get a bench warrant upon us. Mrs. Youngblood and Mrs. Tiers were not very good friends after that."

Willard Titus, the innkeeper who employed the man

with whom Maria had consorted, had a low opinion of the
state's star witness. "Morris Vernoy was barkeeper for
me, and he has kept out of the way for fear of being
subpoenaed on this trial," said Titus. "I have known
Maria Bodine by reputation for five or six years. Her
general moral character has been bad, and where she was
personally concerned or interested, I would not believe
her under oath. She was frequently absent from Walden.
She often came down by the stage which I run, from
Newburgh to New York, for three or four weeks at a time,
and would return back by my stage."

If the tenth day was rough on Maria's reputation, the
eleventh session shattered it. Dr. Thomas Millspaugh,
after testifying that he had treated Maria for four or
five years in the upstate village, tossed the match into the
powder keg. "She told me she was in the family way, or
thought she was," said the doctor. "She also told me the
young man's name, but I shall not give it unless counsel
directs me. [Counsel did not.] I examined her, and found
an enlargement of the breasts and a discoloration around
the nipple called the areola. She had the appearance of a
pregnant woman. I attended her at Mr. Cook's until she
left for Ramapo. She said she had the gonorrhoea."

A juror asked if he believed the woman's ailment was
that.

"She told me she had connexion with some men who had
given it to her," replied the physician. "I afterwards
examined her with my brother, Dr. Gouverneur Millspaugh."

"From this examination had you any doubts as to her
disease?" he was asked.

"I supposed it to be syphilis," said the doctor. "I think
I did not communicate my opinion to her."

District Attorney McKeon subjected the young physician to intensive grilling, seeking to shake his story, some of the questions tending to insinuate that the physician might have tried to pick up a sum of money by involving himself in the Bodine case. Dr. Millspaugh retained his composure and was finally excused.

All through these court sessions Mme. Restell sat at the defense counsel table, occasionally whispering to Brady or Graham, but giving no outward sign of pleasure or displeasure at the testimony. Her lips were held in a straight line, as was her custom, her face immobile, and only her dark eyes revealed her distaste for the proceedings. Once, however, late in the evening of the twelfth day, even the accused woman had to smile, while everyone else roared with laughter. It came during the questioning of a state witness, John B. Hendricks, a carpenter, who kept Cook's cotton mill in repair. One day, he said, Cook asked him to do some carpentry at his house, and on this occasion he saw Maria Bodine.

"Had you ever known Maria Bodine before?" asked Brady during cross-examination.

"No, sir," said Hendricks, adding a non sequitur, "she was going about the house."

"Did she look well or look ill?"

"That's going a leetle beyond my practice, sir."

The audience rocked with laughter.

"I repeat the question," said Brady sternly.

"She looked well and healthy with one exception. That was that she looked from her face and eyes in a pregnant state, and I was never mistaken about such signs."

"Are you married?"

"Yes, sir."

"How many children?"

"There was 12 living when I left last night."

The court stenographer duly noted in the record that there was "great laughter."

On the following days a long procession of witnesses took the stand, most of them residents of Walden and Ramapo. Some had a high opinion of Maria Bodine and a low opinion of Dr. Thomas Millspaugh. Others held the reverse opinions.

Sylvanus Clyman was one of these. He said he'd believe Maria if she made a statement but thought her reputation for virtue was rather down-at-the-heels. "I have known Dr. Millspaugh from a boy," he said. "He was rather wild in his youthful days, but I have never heard much against his moral character, and I would believe him under oath. His character is about as good as the general run in Walden, and they are as good as the generality of people."

Moses Smith, another neighbor, put the matter tersely. "I live in Montgomery. I have known Maria Bodine. Her general character as a virgin is not very good of late."

Others paraded before the jury, speaking their lines, pro and con, until finally the jurors let the court know that they thought there had been enough of this type of testimony and were growing weary of it.

On the fourteenth day—it was by now late on Saturday night—counsel examined and cross-examined a number of medical men on technical points and then agreed to call no more witnesses. The court, more than a little relieved, adjourned the trial to the following Monday.

GUILTY AS CHARGED

James Brady's summation was like a dramatic symphony
—a daylong marshaling of arguments against conviction.
There were legalistic digressions with references to how
the courts of England would rule on certain matters,
bitter commentaries upon the secrecy of the district attorney's office in withholding information before trial,
and rhetorical excursions embroidered by fancy phrases
and biblical references.

One point he stressed dealt with Maria Bodine's refusal
to answer the question whether she had a venereal disease
when she went to work for Joseph Cook. The defense attorney raised the question whether Maria had been seduced, insinuating that perhaps it was the woman who
was the seducer. It was this subject that supplied the
springboard for a statement of his own views on the moral
differences between the sexes.

"There is an idea prevailing that I do not hold the
character of woman in as high an estimate as my fellow
men," he said. "I beg permission to set myself right by
asserting the contrary, and if a strict investigation was

made, it would perhaps be found that I like them too much. I believe that woman and Christianity are the only things that keep men from devouring each other like wolves. I believe if there be anything humanizing on the face of the earth—anything which prevents men from becoming wolves and tigers and preying on each other—it is woman. But I say this—there is an essential difference between women and men—in this respect, that woman may be destroyed forever in that in which a man may be good."

Brady said men seldom committed perjury.

"Take a bad man, put him on the stand, and as long as he had one feeling of a man, ask him if he is willing to immure you in a State prison, and he will say no," said the defense attorney. "He will lie to take away your money from you, but that he will not do. With women it is different. When they part with their chastity, disgrace and infamy follow them through life. If a woman should be false to her marriage vows, she will have her paramour at her side, and will pollute the presence of her lord and master by him. Such is not the character of man. However false he may be, he will never do this. In this respect they differ, because chastity is the basis of character in one instance, and when that departs, no reliance can be placed in her that loses it."

Before the state opened its summation, everyone went out to a nearby tavern for dinner, almost as if the court officers and the witnesses realized that the time was fast approaching when the government would not be paying for any meals. Those not on the payroll must have been infected by the others' enthusiasm.

In his closing statement to the jury District Attorney McKeon spoke for some time about the indictment, the action of the grand jury, and other points at law. Then he drove to the heart of the matter—whether Maria Bodine was, in fact, a reliable witness.

"I presume I shall be told that our witness is a woman of bad character," he said. "The counsel begins by requiring of me a pure and unsullied female to go on that stand and testify against the prisoner. This, I know, you know, we all know, cannot be done. He then assails the woman who has lost her virtue, and asks me as public prosecutor, to bring corroborative testimony of a positive character. How am I to do this? Will others, who have been subjected to the same treatment as herself voluntarily come forward and testify against her? Am I to go down to that den on Greenwich Street, to find other fiendlike beings for this purpose? Am I to take inmates of worse than a brothel to prove what I desire?

"Is it to be Madame Restell's servants that I must take for that purpose? Why, gentlemen, do you for a moment suppose that Madame Restell is the woman who would allow any of her servants to be present and witness her operations? Not she; I say there is not a human heart who could stand by and see the writhing agonies of those who are operated upon. Who is there but Restell and her victim in the room at the time of the operation? No one! We are not to believe that she allows any being to witness it. She who knows the law so well takes good care to manage this part of the business, and when the poor victims leave her den, mark what she says to them by way of caution— 'Speak not of it to anyone; be silent; be quiet; for the act will consign both of us to the State prison.' "

The prosecutor then gave a résumé of the testimony as to Maria's credibility and gleefully asserted that his adversaries had been able to find only five persons in all Orange County who would not believe her under oath. Late in the evening he asked for a conviction on all counts.

On the sixteenth day David Graham, associate counsel for the defense, took up the entire session with a learned argument based upon legal precedents. It was technical, boring, and wearisome to judge and jurors alike. Accounts in the day's papers reflected this tedium. One reporter said the lawyer covered the same ground as his associate and another wrote that his argument on the relative legality of felony versus manslaughter charges "took him a long time to explain." The jurors were restless, and patently eager to see this discourse come to a close. The men who had been so obviously interested in the physical appearance of a pregnant woman's bosom asked not a question about the law and its interpretation.

If the legalistic maneuvering was tiresome to some in the courtroom, it failed to dispel the interest that existed out in town. The next morning, on the seventeenth day of the trial, Ogden Hoffman, special counsel for the prosecution, opened his summation, according to one newspaper, "before as many persons as the court could well contain, without being on each other's heads." Hoffman argued that even if Maria Bodine had "died and passed away from the world" other testimony in the case would suffice to convict Mme. Restell: "We find this poor girl in Restell's splendid house, domiciliated there as one of the family, in a larger house than she ever before resided in. Was she residing there for the purpose of consulting about her monthly turns?" asked Hoffman. "Did that woman receive the poor vagrant into her house, and support her, for the purpose of administering medicine to her? Would not one moment's consultation have enabled her to prescribe for her? The gentleman [McCann] says she stayed there for the purpose of consulting about her turns. If she stayed there for that, where did the money come from? Did she get it from charity? No one had any motive to give that money but the father of the child which was destroyed, whoever he was."

The district attorney's assistant answered the defense contention that Maria had, in fact, been an accomplice of Mme. Restell. "Is this poor girl engaged with Restell for a common purpose and for a common benefit?" he asked the jurors. "Why, it is almost an abuse of terms to say she was. To call her—this poor victim, who is hardly able to drag her trembling form on the stand—to call her the accomplice of the accused, is idle. Why, it is like the lamb being the accomplice of the butcher!

"The gentlemen [the defense counsel] say 'How singular it is Restell never asked her for what purpose she came, and that the witness never told her she wanted an abortion, but that Restell at once said "$75 is my price." "What does this prove? It proves that the house was so notorious she knew that there could have been but one motive in coming there. Does the woman who keeps a house of prostitution ask the girl who goes there what she comes for?"

Hoffman said nothing about how paradoxical it was that such a den of evil should be so notorious and still not bring the wrath of the city administration down upon it. That would have been more than a digression; it would have been an admission that something was rotten in Denmark; that year after year nothing had been done until this complaining witness's story had been laid upon the mayor's desk by a shocked physician in faraway Orange County.

As the session wore on, Hoffman became more and more prolix, and relied more often on the purple phrase to make his point. He said the defense held that although the testimony shows "the broken victim issuing from the door, that Madame Restell did not do the deed." It was

all Hoffman needed to turn for inspiration to Shakespeare's *Henry VI:*

> *Who finds the heifer dead, and bleeding fresh,*
> *And sees fast by a butcher with an ax,*
> *But will suspect 'twas he that made the slaughter?*
> *Who finds the partridge in the puttock's nest,*
> *But may imagine how the bird was dead,*
> *Although the kite soar with unbloodied beak?*

Carried away by his own words, Hoffman quoted from
Scripture, from the lives of Henry VIII and Bloody
Mary, and from several textbooks on midwifery.

"Think, in God's name," he concluded, "think of the
responsibility of what you are about to do. The public
look to you; the eyes of your fellow-citizens are riveted
on you, your motives, and your deeds. The eye of outraged humanity is keenly watching you, and on you are
centered the hopes and fears of the best and the noblest in
the land." As Hoffman sat down the courtroom burst into
loud applause, which the officers of the court could not
quell for some minutes.

Perhaps because he desired to ease the jury's task,
Judge Scott delivered a charge to the jury that was
succinct, short, and easy to understand. He made the
point that "it is usually impracticable to obtain absolute
certainty in human affairs" but that reasonable certainty
could be accepted in its place. He then gave the case to
the jury.

It was 7:00 P.M. and at eight o'clock an officer announced that the twelve men had agreed upon a verdict.

Richard Venables, the hosiery merchant, who had sat
through seventeen days of testimony, spoke for the jury.
The verdict was unanimous, and held that Mme. Restell

was guilty of a misdemeanor. The felony charges went by the board.

By this time the evening was well along and as it was unlikely bail could be produced, the prisoner was committed to prison for the night and court adjourned until eleven o'clock the next morning.

Before dawn on Thursday, November 11, a queue of curious men had lined up, waiting to get seats in the courtroom. The *National Police Gazette* reported that the chamber was "crowded to excess" before the judge and jurors even reached the courthouse.

Just before noon Mme. Restell was brought from the city prison, where she had spent an uncomfortable night. Accompanied by her husband, she took her usual seat at the defense counsel table, looking at no one and speaking to no one. The *Gazette* recorded for posterity that "she was elegantly dressed in a rich black silk gown, handsomely trimmed black velvet mantilla, white satin bonnet, and wore a large, heavy lace veil."

Everyone could see that she looked excessively pale as Mr. Graham argued against returning the prisoner to jail for twenty-four hours and for an arrest of judgment. The court was not moved by the lawyer's appeal. "I do not see why any difference should be made in this case," the judge said bluntly. "Why, every day some poor devil is brought up here and sent off to the State prison without ceremony, probably because he has no counsel, although the Court always assigns counsel if possible, and I have no idea that there should be one law for one individual and another law for another. This woman is the same as any other woman convicted of a similar crime, and we can make no distinction. The Court has decided,— to prevent any difficulty that may arise in this case from delay; so that the whole of the proceedings might have to be gone over again; in view of the vast expense to which the public have been put and the length of time the trial has occupied—to proceed at once and pass sentence. Mr. Clerk, arraign the prisoner."

Graham interrupted to say that he had advised the prisoner, when asked why judgment should not be passed, to claim that the court had no legal right to do so. But the clerk did ask the question after requesting that Mme. Restell stand, and the defendant remained mute, whereupon the judge sentenced her.

"Caroline Lohman, alias Madame Restell," said Judge Scott (omitting her usual given name, Anna), "you have been convicted by a jury of the county of a misdemeanor in procuring a miscarriage, and the Court sentences you to be imprisoned for one year in the penitentiary on Blackwell's Island, that being the extent of your punishment prescribed by the law for the offence of which you have been found guilty."

With few exceptions, those in the jammed courtroom jumped to their feet and started to applaud, but the clerks and bailiffs moved swiftly to restore order. Whatever Mme. Restell felt about the sentence was hidden behind the veil that cheated the audience of any emotional titillation. Court officers led her away to the city prison to await hearings on an application for a writ of error and a stay of execution of sentence, and so the eighteenth day of the unusually long, but "wonderful" trial of the abortionist came to an end.

Four days later a judge of the appellate division decided that had the verdict been one given on the felony charges he would have had power to grant a stay, but as the prisoner had been found guilty only of a misdemeanor, he had no such power. Four days after that Mme. Restell was taken from the city prison to begin her term in the grim penitentiary on Blackwell's Island in the East River.

After its Roman holiday, the city settled down to its old routine, not to be awakened again for several days. Even so, New Yorkers found the newsstands and cigar store counters loaded down with hastily printed pamphlets containing the full transcript of the trial. Printers and pamphleteers had worked overtime to get the little booklets out at the earliest moment. Most of them were issued in fine print to conserve paper and were excruciatingly difficult to read, but they were bought up by the thousands, most of them selling for a shilling. All in all, it was a great coup for journalistic enterprise.

Respectable citizens who would have shuddered at far less explicit words and terms in a novel read the pamphlets avidly, secure in the assumption that it was perfectly correct to learn just what was said during Mme. Restell's trial. Men read them in their clubs; women secreted them in closets to read when husbands were at work and children at school. And more than one youngster, feeling the first twinges of sexual development, stole away to attic or woodshed to experience new thrills.

Over on Blackwell's Island, Mme. Restell was out of circulation for twelve months. She had had nothing to do with the publications, but she could not have devised a better way to keep her name, and practice, in the public eye.

No one in those days thought of interviewing the individual jurors about their verdict. The community had seen justice done, at least the brand of justice they supported. That Mme. Restell was punished for doing what hundreds of women—and presumably their male lovers, legal or illegal—wanted done caused no stir in New York's society. People then believed the best place for such doings was under the rug, swept there by a common hypocrisy.

Yet there may have been some trembling and apprehension lest the abortionist make public her list of customers, but the prisoner was too smart to risk this revenge. After all, she would be out of prison in a year. If she let such secrets out of the bag she could hardly expect to get new clients when she reopened her offce.

It was unfair. She paid a price while others involved in the same business went free. It was neither the first nor the last time that such an injustice would be done in the name of morality.

LADIES IN TROUBLE

It was a forbidding place, the old penitentiary on Blackwell's Island. No prison is a pleasant place but this grim edifice, stuck away in the middle of the river between Manhattan and Queens, had a desolate appearance heightened by the very fact it was only a few thousand feet from midtown New York. Had it been in a deep forest, or even on the snow-swept Russian steppes, it would not have seemed so ugly.

Today the prison is gone. To reach the apartments, hospitals, and medical institutions that have taken the old fortress's place, visitors now use an elevator leading down from the Queensboro Bridge that sweeps high across the river, straddling the island, and, when it is operating, a cable car. In Mme. Restell's day, access was achieved by using a ferryboat.

The abortionist was removed to the penitentiary and given a cell in the women's section. For a time she was almost forgotten—except possibly by pregnant women who had to look elsewhere for someone to save them from bearing a love child.

If the notorious prisoner was forgotten by the general public, she was not by her friends, some of them influential members of the city government. As soon as the hullabaloo over the trial had died down and it was deemed safe to take steps in her behalf, conditions in her cell improved markedly.

The dirty, lumpy mattress stuffed with musty straw was thrown out and in its place appeared a fancy new featherbed as comfortable as any in the better houses in the city. Two easy chairs replaced the usual bench without a back, a rocker was supplied, a carpet brought in to hide the cold stone floor, and other furnishings later described as "elegant." The cubicle was transformed into a pleasant boudoir.

At night a light was left on in the lady's cell. This was a flagrant transgression of penal regulations, but no one dared object. After a few weeks, the cell door was left open at all times, allowing the lady "physician" to move about the institution at will. It was never divulged whether she had access to other areas on the island or, indeed, whether at times she actually left her prison.

Such latitude was not impossible. It is known that half a century ago a small-time gangster named Joey Rao was incarcerated on the island and enjoyed remarkable privileges. At the time (the early 1930s) Tammany Hall, which controlled the Democratic political machine in New York, was riding high—so high that Fiorello LaGuardia was elected on a reform ticket to throw the rascals out. The "Little Flower" appointed a professional penologist, Austin McCormick, as commissioner of correction, and almost at once the new prison chief learned that conditions on Welfare Island—its new name—needed airing and reform.

Within two or three weeks of LaGuardia's swearing in,

Commissioner McCormick led a raid on the institution, using 100 policemen. As the raiders passed each gate and barrier, they cut the telephone wires to prevent word of their presence from being flashed ahead. They found immediate and tragic evidence that ordinary prisoners were suffering from abuse and malnutrition, but when they reached the prison barber shop the raiders found a scene straight out of the *Arabian Nights*.

Joey Rao, clad in a rainbow-hued silk lounging robe, was seated in a reclining barber's chair which served as his throne, from which he issued the orders for running the penitentiary. The warden was nothing but a spineless figurehead. Lolling at the foot of the "throne" was a huge German police dog, which victims told the commissioner was often loosed against recalcitrant prisoners and guards.

In the cabinets that once held razors, soaps, and other tonsorial aids, Rao had a superior collection of liquors and wines. On the windowsill outside was a dovecote where homing pigeons were housed. The birds had been used to smuggle heroin into the gangster's throne room from "the mainland."

Once the guards' tongues were loosened, they told McCormick that Rao had made a daily check of newly arrived prisoners. When he found friends or worthy followers, such "fresh fish" were given better cells and many privileges. Once when a French chef was jailed for beating his wife, the gangland chief ordered him to prepare gourmet meals for himself and his henchmen. The best cuts of meat, the freshest vegetables, and other good food were removed from the kitchen at the other prisoners' expense, and served up with fancy sauces in the throne room.

Women prisoners also came under Rao's scrutiny and the youngest and prettiest often found it wiser to accept his overtures than to refuse and be mistreated for their independence. During the investigation that followed these incredible disclosures it was revealed that on many occasions Rao had left the island at night for a party in the city or for meetings with mobsters in Manhattan hotels.

While Mme. Restell's illegal privileges didn't reach the high mark set by the gifted inmate who followed her years later, she was blessed with many favors. She may have left the island, too, for all that is known. If she did not dare take this risk there were certain other arrangements that made her incarceration much less arduous. Visiting hours were altered for her benefit and her husband was permitted to spend as much time with her as she desired. One newspaper reported later that the warden, Jacob Acker, allowed her husband to visit her at will and that "he [Lohman] would remain alone with her as long as suited his or her pleasure."

By one means or another Mme. Restell endured her year's sentence without too much trauma. Poor Warden Acker paid a heavy penalty for his collusion with the abortionist. Because he had betrayed the trust placed in him by an austere and rather puritanical administration, he was haled up on charges, tried before the board of aldermen, and bounced out of his post.

The day Mme. Restell was released was memorable too. She stepped off the ferryboat onto the soil of Manhattan with all the aplomb of a returning hero. Her carriage, with driver and footman, was waiting for her and she got in to the rousing applause of a small group of citizens who either remembered she would be freed that day or had been tipped off by prison employees.

Completely unabashed by her experience—which, after all, had been far short of horrible—the abortionist announced her return to society by stating publicly that her trial and imprisonment were easily worth $100,000 to her in advertising. Her estimate was probably on the low side.

Bolder than ever after a year away from business, the female "physician" found the old place on Greenwich Street no longer to her liking. Fruit and vegetable wholesalers were moving into the lower West Side district and Mme. Restell did not like the idea of her clientele walking through decaying vegetables or slipping on overripe fruit. She began a search for new quarters.

She found what she wanted at 160 Chambers Street and soon was ensconced in larger and better rooms. Chambers Street crossed most of Manhattan Island directly to the north of the grounds occupied by the City Hall. There were law offices all around her, as the courts were only a block or two away, and she thought the neighborhood immeasurably more chic than her first address.

Perhaps Mme. Restell remembered how much the illegal furnishings had improved her prison cell. At any rate, she decorated the new offices and home with what could certainly be called opulent splendor.

Her parlor, or waiting room, was done in the heavy-handed style of the period, replete with flowered carpeting, tasseled curtains, steel engravings, and an ormolu mantel clock. There were several bedrooms, equally well furnished, on the upstairs floors besides the one she shared in legal domesticity with the ex-printer from the *Herald*. Lohman had given up his job in the composing room of the morning paper, realizing he could make greater profits aiding and abetting his wife in her several lines of endeavor. He also decided to go into the mail-order business, and quickly won his wife's approval. Whether it was because of his former connection with a newspaper or just his canny nature, his devotion to advertising became sincere and undiluted.

He initiated an advertising campaign, first in his wife's behalf, then later for himself, that proved unbelievably successful. Bishop Huntington, who wrote a small pamphlet on the abortionist more than a century ago, stated that one daily newspaper alone accepted more than $20,000 in advertising from her in a single year. In today's world, when soap, auto, and cigarette manufacturers assign millions to this type of promotion, $20,000 may appear small potatoes, but when Mme. Restell was putting her ads in the papers eggs sold for six cents a dozen and decent apartments could be rented for $5 and $6 a month.

A lot of people were spending money as if the use of it were about to go out of style. The whole country was caught up in a fever of expansionism. Settlers were pushing westward across the prairies, seeking new and free land for homesteads. By the time Mme. Restell had been out of prison less than two years the *New York Tribune* was reporting that 19,339 New Yorkers had quit the city for the California gold fields. Ship lines were vying for much of this traffic as it was easier for a would-be gold hunter to take a ship from New York to the Isthmus of Panama, cross that narrow strip of land, and take passage in another vessel up the Pacific coast than to risk the dangers of hunger, thirst, and Indian attacks on the overland route across the western plains.

Several months after the *Tribune* revealed how the gold rush fever had smitten residents of the city, that paper and others ran stories of how a steam locomotive had pulled the first train from New York to Peekskill. That was in September of 1849 and a few months later the New York and Harlem Railroad was given a franchise to lay tracks clear down to Chambers Street, the very street where Mme. Restell now had her home.

New York in 1850 had a police force of 900 men, a fact that made most residents very proud. What with crime in the streets on the increase and other serious problems, policemen had little time to bother with the likes of Mme. Restell. Unless the situations with which they had to cope were extremely aggravated, they followed the rule of "live and let live." For the abortionist at 160 Chambers Street, it was a highly satisfactory philosophy.

A simple mathematical process suggests that if the female "physician" could spend $20,000 annually in advertising she must have had a steady stream of patients coming to her door. Though most of them chose to visit the place under cover of darkness, the patrolmen pounding the beat must have been aware of what was going on. Just as obviously, the higher-ups in the department were exerting no pressure on the men putting in long hours walking the sidewalks of lower Manhattan. A daily paper explained all this in an editorial that ran soon after Mme. Restell moved: "She held in her keeping the dread secrets of many a high-toned family, and fear of exposure led these people quickly to defend her when she got into the toils."

Perhaps these "high-toned" families *did* exert influence on the police, but it is more likely that it was a matter of laissez-faire, with the constabulary seeing no urgent reason to interfere with a system that had its supporters and its justification.

There is no record to fix the date, but about this time, while the abortionist was growing richer at her nocturnal practice, her brother, Joseph Trow, left England and joined his sister and brother-in-law in New York. At once Lohman's mail-order business skyrocketed. Mme. Restell's hubsand, with no formal education and nothing but his experience as a printer to go on, assumed the flowery alias of "Dr. Moreceau," supposedly a wise and eminent French expert at treating female maladies. Trow and "Dr. Moreceau" expanded their advertising in the New York papers and then began placing their announcements in magazines far afield from the city. They claimed that they could send purchasers "infallible remedies" for female complaints. Through innuendo that was not at all subtle, they made it clear that these pills would be beneficial in terminating unwanted pregnancies.

It was roughly at this point in history that Mr. Barnum expounded his famous thesis that a sucker is born every minute, and the men at 160 Chambers Street proved he was right. Women sent in their $5 and $10 orders from all parts of the East and the partners in Mme. Restell's basement sent out their "infallible" nostrums. When the ladies—already in abject panic over their delicate condition—tasted the pills, they discovered they were nothing but bread dough rolled into small pellets and flavored with anise or peppermint. The liquids they received in the mail were nothing but water made evil-tasting to cover their worthlessness and tinted with vegetable coloring.

There was no recourse to the Post Office Department, which looked the other way. Very few women took even this small step to rectify the swindle because, having been victimized, they did not want to reveal their motive or expose themselves to public ridicule.

The middle years of the nineteenth century were bonanza years for swindlers, fakers, and illicit mail-order establishments. Almost anything could be advertised. One common swindle was based on an advertisement offering to send an excellent steel engraving of the father of this country in return for $1. When the unwary swallowed this come-on and sent the money, they received a penny postage stamp, then carrying a very fine steel engraving of George Washington. Another swindle was based upon womankind's historic desire to be curvaceous and attractive. The offer was for a bust developer and was aimed especially at less well-endowed women and growing girls anxious to hasten maturity. Varying sums were cited in the many advertisements but the commonest called for $5. The unfortunate women, already miserable over their lack of physical attributes, discovered when they opened their return mail that there was nothing in the envelope except a drawing of a man's hand.

The daily papers of the period did not hesitate to carry advertisements of abortionists, knowing that the innocent words in the announcements cloaked harsher meanings. In most papers the ads were strung one after another, offering considerable choice to women in trouble. The relative merits of the practitioners could not be determined from the advertisements. That was achieved by gossip and word-of-mouth boasting. The small notices read like these:

A CURE FOR LADIES IMMEDIATELY. Doctor Smith's Female Antidote. Never fails. Certain to produce desired results in twenty-four hours. No injurious results.

IMPORTANT TO WOMEN. Dr. Jones (30 years' experience) guarantees certain relief to married ladies at one visit with or without medicine.

LADIES IN TROUBLE. Experienced physician offers certain relief with tried-and-true French medicine. Not injurious to health. Nurses on hand at all times.

Some of the advertisements insinuated that electrical intervention was the secret device that would terminate unwanted pregnancies. Electricity was a magic word, hardly understood by scientists themselves, and was used carelessly by many manufacturers of cures for baldness, rheumatism, sciatica, and "lost manhood." It was only natural that quacks would use it in their advertisements aimed at the women referred to as "in trouble."

If Mme. Restell had been content with modest riches, she might have relied on her husband's and brother's mail-order business. They were making handsome profits of 80 percent on their investment. It was a far better return than those from gold mine stocks or speculating in western land. But greed drove her to continue, and except for a minor brush with the law, she escaped punishment for nearly thirty years more.

Although she was the most notorious abortionist in town, was by no means alone in the field. Many accredited physicians turned to abortion when their rich patients offered large enough financial inducements to tempt them. It was common practice for these doctors to assure their patients that their personally compounded pills and syrups would bring on a miscarriage, although they knew that the medicines seldom had the desired effect. When a woman found that the pills were worthless she went to the same doctor for an illegal operation, knowing that he was already privy to her secret.

Several of these medical men opened "lying-in asylums," supposedly for women awaiting delivery of wanted children; but they were not averse to using the institutions as places to perform abortions and give aftercare. Midwives, too, worked both sides of the street, lured by the higher fees they could squeeze from patients by abortions. In numbers, these practitioners probably ranked highest on the list of illegal abortionists simply because women in trouble often preferred to reveal their secret to one of their own sex.

As New York's population grew, Mme. Restell benefited by the social ferment of the times. A few years after she reestablished herself following her prison term, the town was caught up in the excitement of the women's rights movement. A convention was held in 1853 at the Broadway Tabernacle at which Lucy Stone, Lucretia Mott, Susan B. Anthony, William Lloyd Garrison, and Wendell Phillips—all prominent in this and other movements—spoke to a crowded house. A year later the United States Inebriate Asylum, first of its kind in the nation, opened its doors, promising to convert drunkards into model family men.

Not all New Yorkers were bending their efforts to improve mankind. Many of the richer inhabitants were caught up in a round of parties, gourmet dinners, fancy dress balls, and receptions. Around the same time the asylum for drunks opened Mrs. William Schermerhorn invited 600 guests to her mansion in what is now the heart of Greenwich Village and instructed them to dress like members of the court of Louis XV. It took a great deal of persuasion on the part of the wives to secure their husbands' consent, but they won the day—or evening—and the men turned up at the function in knee breeches and silken hose, feeling like the foolish fops they were.

Mme. Restell, of course, was never invited to these affairs, but she did not have to read the papers to know what was going on. She heard about the extravaganzas from unwary daughters of the top families. These young ladies, carried away by the music and champagne, often succumbed to masculine wiles and left the parties for rendezvous in sequestered apartments and hotel rooms. Their indiscretion often led to pregnancy.

By now word had gotten around that the place at 160 Chambers Street was one of the safest repositories for dark secrets. The abortionist naturally took advantage of the situation and raised her fees—far beyond what had been charged the ignorant country girl Maria Bodine —to anywhere from $500 to $1,000. She knew the financial standing of the prominent families in town and fashioned a sliding scale of payments based on that knowledge.

Coincident with the craze for fancy balls among the socially elite there was an aversion to large families, and Mme. Restell proudly let it be known that much of the credit for holding the population down among the well-to-do belonged to her. No one disputed her claim.

It has always been a commonplace in New York City that respectability and crime can exist within a block or two of each other. Mme. Restell's establishment on Chambers Street was west of Broadway but quite close to City Hall Park. About the same distance to the east and a little to the north of City Hall was an intersection of streets then known all over the world as "the toughest street corner on earth." It was Five Points, a sinkhole of vice and crime, infested with thieves, gamblers, prostitutes, fences for stolen goods, procurers, and people too poor to move away. Cellars without ventilation were used as boarding rooms and occupied by members of both sexes, most of them drunkards, dope addicts, and prostitutes.

Policemen never entered the district except in pairs, and then only under severe necessity.

In the center of this hellhole, as we saw, was an open space called, with sinister effrontery, Paradise Square, on one side of which stood the Old Brewery. This slum warren was home to many men who belonged to a collection of rowdies called the Dead Rabbits who terrorized the lower East Side by day and by night.

An ex-New Orleans gambler, "Captain" Isaiah Rynders, moved to New York in the 1850s and quickly sensed how valuable the Dead Rabbits could be if used as a political force. Gaining control of them by supplying plenty of whiskey and by offering protection from the law, Rynders welded the members into a group that exercised incredible power.

Big, handsome Mayor Fernando Wood, who knew a good thing when he saw it, backed "Captain" Rynders in disputes with other gangs and with reformers. The Mayor, twisting the ends of his luxuriant black mustache, granted Rynders's Park Row saloon endless immunities and looked the other way as the old southern gambler opened casinos and houses of ill repute.

The Common Council was strict about enforcing the law that policemen "take charge of any and all swine at large" and see them put in the pound until paid for by their owners, but it blinked at real graft and crime. Even the *Herald*, which could overlook monstrous examples of evil if it suited the publisher, criticized the police commissioner for ordering newsboys to quit hawking papers on Sundays. This brave order, said the paper, "is not the closing of gambling dens, for they are still in full blast, nor a finishing edict against the houses of ill fame."

Safe behind the mayor's protection, Rynders turned

the Dead Rabbits loose in an epidemic of looting, thieving, gang fighting, and political oppression. A rival gang leader of the Bowery Boys was murdered in his favorite saloon and then all hell broke loose. For weeks the streets of downtown New York were torn by rifle shots, bricks tossed through windows, and bareknuckle fighting involving hundreds of toughs.

The lid was off. Rioting continued for months. Neither Mayor Wood nor the council intervened, while the city police adopted a hands-off attitude. Then in 1857 the legislature in Albany, strongly Republican, took the step Tammany Hall feared. It amended the city charter, abolished the city police force, and set up another, called the Metropolitan Police District, under commissioners to be appointed by the governor. Mayor Wood refused to disband "his" police department.

Whereas up to this time the main belligerents had been the Dead Rabbits and the Bowery Boys, now the warfare involved the municipal versus the metropolitan police. There was a bloody battle between the law officers, starting near Five Points, shifting to Chambers Street hard by Mme. Restell's establishment, and winding up at City Hall. The poor women awaiting normal deliveries or recovering from abortions at the place on Chambers Street heard the firing and shouting and had reason more than ever to regret that they had turned to the female "physician" in their hour of peril.

Suddenly there was silence. Firing stopped all over downtown New York. Mme. Restell's maids peeked out through the heavy curtains and saw uniformed men of the Seventh Regiment, guns at the ready, marching into the park around City Hall. Mayor Wood submitted to arrest, but that did not ease the tension. The dispute dragged along in the courts, and the police of both forces continued to pound their beats and each other instead of combining to fight the city's gangs.

Things came to a head on the Fourth of July. While decent citizens were watching fireworks displays after nightfall, the Dead Rabbits, armed with guns, sticks, and dornicks, erupted from Five Points and launched an attack on the headquarters of their arch rivals, the Bowery Boys. All night long the streets of lower Manhattan resembled those of a city at war. Homes were pillaged, citizens bludgeoned, and fires started at a dozen sites.

In the small hours of the morning the thugs went home to rest but the next afternoon, refreshed and rearmed, they sortied into the streets again, this time attacking policemen regardless of whether they belonged to the outlawed city force or the new "Metropolitan District."

In desperation, the commissioners appointed by the governor pleaded with "Captain" Rynders to quell the rioting, and the ex-gambler did try to get his boys back into Five Points. But by now they had tasted enough blood to want more and they paid him no heed. Finally, he admitted defeat and advised the authorities to call out every soldier in town. Hours later, as midnight approached, two regiments of militia, supported by the Metropolitan Police, slogged through the rubble-strewn streets around lower Broadway, the Bowery, Chambers Street, and Park Row. When they had finished their task, the thugs and plug-uglies of both gangs had been driven back into their slum warrens and the city drew a gigantic breath of relief.

The city still could boast of only 800,000 inhabitants and although the Astor House, the Metropolitan, and other hotels, as well as the homes of the well-to-do, were ornate beyond belief, the new science of sanitation had wrought little change. Cattle and sheep were still driven into town to be slaughtered at abattoirs on the river banks. Some came down from Connecticut and upper New York State through Westchester and the Bronx, while others were brought to Jersey points and ferried across to a Manhattan landing near 125th Street.

Smallpox and yellow fever rivaled typhoid as killers of old and young alike. Milk was handled in open cans from carts that wandered about the dirty streets collecting germs between sales, and outdoor privies were behind all but the very finest houses in town. The "honey wagon," which collected human waste, was a common sight everywhere, and the system for supplying water was a hodgepodge of municipal piping and private wells, many of them unsafe because of bad drainage.

Considering the enormous lack of knowledge about infection and public health, it was a wonder that more of Mme. Restell's patients did not die from puerperal fever, blood poisoning, and other diseases. The women who submitted to the abortionist's ministrations went into her establishment with the odds heavily against them. It was only by chance—and the fact that most of them were young—that any lived through the ordeal.

"AS MANY PROSTITUTES
AS METHODISTS"

One Sunday morning a bishop of the Methodist Episcopal Church, saddened by events of the 1850s and early 1860s, waited for his congregation to settle down and then startled them with a statement that was soon echoed in papers from the Atlantic to the Pacific and even abroad. "There are as many prostitutes plying their trade in this wicked city," he told the parishioners of St. Paul's Church, "as there are Methodists listed on our church rolls."

This was either a sad confession that Methodism had fallen on bad days since those of John Wesley and George Whitefield, or it meant that ladies of the evening were thicker on the streets of the Tenderloin, Chelsea, and Broadway areas than fleas on an old hound's back. Ecclesiastical authorities having been consulted, it was soon learned that the latter was true. In fact, the women of easy virtue constituted a very large and easily visible fragment of the city's population.

As if to refute the good bishop, Police Superintendent John A. Kennedy sent his bluecoats out with pencils and pads and compiled a census intended to show that New York was not in fact a rival of Paris, London, or Constantinople, as had been charged. But his statistics lowered nobody's fever of anxiety, certainly not a reformer's. There were only 621 houses of prostitution, only 99 houses of assignation, and a mere 75 concert-hall saloons rated as being of evil repute—hardly cause to be exercised, in Kennedy's opinion.

But public opinion was exercised. Reformers preached red-hot sermons; meetings were held in Cooper Union to alert a citizenry that already knew more than enough of the facts. Politicians, for once, kept silent, not wishing to lose votes by jumping on the bandwagon: They knew how short the memories of angry voters are.

No one had to define the houses of ill repute or the assignation houses. They were like those all over the world. But the concert-hall saloons were something of an innovation in New York. The city was actually overrun with them. These dives were all-purpose haunts of pleasure, many of them alluring, thanks to the "pretty waiter-girls" who radiated charm and drew by the thousands bums and thieves, clerks and well-to-do businessmen and slumming out-of-towners.

Most of these places were at street level or in basements. All had blazing "transparencies" at their entrances —illuminated drawings and gay broadsides picturing the physical attractions of their current entertainers. *Entertainer* was a word to be used with casual abandon.

The primary duty of the waiter-girls was to rush the steins of beer or glasses of hard liquor to the customers. But they also sang a little and danced a little, and at some of the larger establishments they joined together with a few unfortunate actors who were "between jobs" to stage short playlets. In the midst of these chores they were expected to make the male customers happy, which consisted for the most part of sitting in their laps and submitting to clumsy drunken embraces.

One thing about the waiter-girls never differed: Their uniform of the day—or of the evening, rather—was always the same: bare legs above red-tasseled red boots; a very short skirt like a mini-mini or ballerina's tutu and a tight bodiced upper garment with a daringly low neckline. The term "neckline," to be honest, was a misnomer, anatomically speaking: it was a bust line, for professional reasons. The girls who took these jobs were seldom as pretty as the gaudy transparencies indicated, but one thing they had to be: plump as partridges. They overflowed the costume wherever it came to an end, top or bottom.

Word of all this implied pulchritude naturally went out into the hinterland, whetting the appetites of many men, but a writer on the *New York World* could have disenchanted them. He called the girls "abandoned women" and said the portraits of the girls hung near the entrances "were taken at random from the stock of some photograph dealer, and have no connection whatever with the hags employed in the saloons."

Present-day Playboy Clubs employ some of the same techniques developed by the concert-hall saloons, but only some of them. The abbreviated costumes, the low "bust line," and the shapeliness of the girls hold the same attraction but today's girls are always young and often beautiful. And no one sits in anyone's lap.

Next to the waiter-girls, the busiest people in the saloons were the bartenders. It was nothing for a place to have ten or a dozen men drawing beer or serving hard liquor. The owners of these establishments had to meet only a few requirements: They had to pay off the police, keep customers from murdering one another, and stay in business three or four years. They could then retire and live comfortably forever after on their unbelievable profits.

Down along the waterfront, particularly on Water Street, the saloons were not as fancy. The drinks did not cost as much and the "pretty waiter-girls" were older, less endowed with charm, and clearly evidenced the fact they had been demoted from Broadway to the dock area. In these dives the transparencies were not needed. The appeal to the passing male was much more direct. The girls sat huddled in the windows, just at sidewalk level, their bodices lower than ever or their bosoms fully exposed, like the prostitutes in the cribs of many tropic countries. In bad times it was all a man could do to get past one of these places without being wrestled inside by one or more of the girls.

Most of the saloons—good and bad—had rooms upstairs for the use of customers overwhelmed by bad booze or the "spell" of the waiter-girls. If the management wanted to stay in business, the men enjoyed their evening, paid their bills, and went home in safety. In the low resorts they were often given Mickey Finns, robbed, and thrown out into the alley with nothing on but their underwear. Frequenters of such places were lucky to escape without a broken head.

One point has to be made: the bishops and preachers, the reformers, and those who viewed with alarm did not have to guess at what was going on; it was all out in the open. The paper for which Mme. Restell's husband had worked—the *Herald*—ran column after column of ads for these concert-hall saloons. The owners vied for business in big black type claiming to have the prettiest girls, the most "accomplished" girls, the most "statuesque" girls. Any reader who could not interpret the word *statuesque* did not deserve to enjoy the pleasures in store for him.

Some of the managers even boasted that they kept a corps of agents on the road, perpetually seeking out even more beautiful girls. A few boasted that these scouts frequented the big cities of Europe in their quest for feminine pulchritude. The advertisements made it clear that men of all ages and walks of life were most welcome; but like the movies of today that carry symbols warning off children, they made it clear that "no boys were wanted" in the saloons.

There was another type of institution devoted to fighting the businessman's ennui. It functioned, strangely enough, mostly in the daylight hours. These places were called "cigar store batteries" and, seen from the sidewalk, appeared to be just that. An innocent man, in need of a pocketful of cigars or some pipe tobacco, could step into one of these "stores," make his purchase, and leave without incident, although he would probably discover that the tobacco was stale or bad. The operators of these places were not really interested in peddling smokes.

A man-about-town, familiar with the situation, would excuse himself from his friends, if walking in a group, and step inside, ostensibly to buy a cigar. But he would continue on past the shabby collection of items in the glass counter and ascend a narrow flight of stairs leading into a parlor on the second floor. There, such a man would not be surprised to find two or three ladies clad in rather garish costume or perhaps only in fur-trimmed lingerie. If it suited him, he enjoyed a glass of sherry or claret before making his choice known and disappearing into one

85

of several bedrooms with one of the ladies. If business was pressing or his lunch hour short, he was more direct, not bothering with social amenities.

How these places became known as cigar store "batteries" is a fact lost in the city's ancient history, but they were all located downtown where business houses flanked every street and wives seldom had an excuse for venturing. The "batteries," like today's fast-food shops, were geared to the time and the place and served their customers with expedition and noteworthy efficiency.

The houses of prostitution—the better ones—were located farther uptown. A visitor to New York in the latter half of the twentieth century would never dream that Greene Street was once the gaudiest, bawdiest thoroughfare in a gay and pleasure-oriented city. It is today a street of unassuming loft buildings, where hats, sweaters, and other requisites for the millinery and garment trades are manufactured using assembly-line techniques with high-speed cutters and sewing machines.

Greene Street is a couple of blocks west of Broadway; in the 1850s and 1860s it was an avenue of sin extending from Canal Street north to Eighth Street, now one of the main business streets serving Greenwich Village. By day a hundred and more years ago, the street was nothing to excite the curious. There was one red brick or brownstone house after another, running along both sides, and, if anything, one of the quietest streets in town. Almost all of the inmates were asleep, insuring the peaceful atmosphere of the region. But just as the crooked streets of Montmartre and the alleys of the Vieux Carré come to life with the rising of the moon, so did Manhattan's Greene Street.

Any house not a brothel on Greene Street was an exception. The sin palaces all had big lights over the entrances, most of them red, and there was enough glass to hold the names of the owners or the name by which the house was known to steady customers—such names as Flossie's, Hilda's, or Rusty's; others less personal, such as The Rose Room, the Forget-me-not, or the Sailor's Dock.

No matter how depraved a segment of society may be, it will have its status differences. In Greene Street the higher the number—which meant the farther uptown— the higher the price and the class. Ordinary men frequented the bawdy houses nearer Canal Street, while the trade for the uptown houses arrived often in cabs and hacks, which were instructed to call back for their owners in the small hours of the morning.

No one bothered to make Greene Street appear other than it was—one long string of whorehouses. The police knew all about it. The city officials knew all about it. The churches and the reform elements had no misapprehensions about its existence. It thrived because there was no power that could overcome the lack of interest of the city government and the police. On the other hand, there was no real demand for a cleanup. Most New Yorkers looked upon the brothels as a fact of life, a natural adjunct to a port city's existence, just like the ships tied up at the piers, the sailors' taverns, the ship chandlers' shops, and the Custom House.

Citizens of the city had worked out their own rationalization for the presence of "the houses." Although they knew in their hearts that the customers were men of the town—brokers, realtors, lawyers, merchants, salesmen, and artisans—and not just sailors in from long, lonely weeks far from land, they cloaked their understanding with the myth that the gay blades who frequented Flossie's place and Rusty's house were almost all wanderers from the sea. So Greene Street thrived for the better part of three decades—a noisy sin street where raucous laughter could be heard almost every time a door opened, where the strains of piano music issued from every red-lighted facade, and where hundreds of young women started on the inevitable decline that attends commercial vice.

Some of the madams of these bawdy houses were personable, well-educated women, whose company many a man preferred to that of his own womenfolk. They dressed elegantly in imported silks and cashmeres, served fine wines, and ran their establishments with strict decorum. The houses themselves rivaled those of the town's merchant princes, fitted out sumptuously in the decor of the day.

One of the proprietors had a daughter who was educated in a private finishing school far from the city, grew up, and married without ever knowing how her mother lived in such evident luxury. Josie Woods, another madam, expected her guests to arrive in tails and white tie—and they did. They drank champagne and chatted amiably with the girls, who always appeared garbed in expensive and tasteful evening gowns. Some of these young ladies could converse in French and German, and the rumor mills of the day had it that they made as much as $200 in a night. These same rumor mills claimed that many of the prostitutes married the young bucks who visited them at Flora's or Daphne's house and went on to live lives of respectable affluence. It was a pretty myth, one repeated since the time of the dancing girls on the Nile. The truth was all too often less roseate. Most of the girls lost their looks, moved down Greene Street from one bagnio to another, and wound up sitting in the windows on Water Street, their haggard faces and shrunken bosoms emblems of their downfall.

Two other establishments in New York stood out as rendezvous for the fun-loving set. They had many similarities, and many differences, and each had its coterie of supporters. Harry Hill's concert saloon on Houston Street thrived for twenty years. An ex-pugilist, Hill possessed a character which made men like to go to his place, if only for the excitement—as in some speakeasies of the Prohibition era years later—of being insulted by the proprietor. A visitor from Grand Rapids or Omaha would go to any lengths to avoid going home without visiting Hill's place. It was, in truth, a colorful spectacle. Besides the hundred waiter-girls always on hand, there were judges and lawyers, government officials and prize-fighters, thugs, fences, ward heelers, and many a man whose name was in the lists of the best brokerage house customers.

Hill was a martinet. He had a dozen rules about the behavior of his guests and enforced them rigidly. Anyone who failed to meet the test was usually knocked down and manhandled down the stairs and out onto the sidewalk. Harry Hill boasted that whether his clients were good or evil men, no crime was ever committed inside the walls of his saloon. What happened outside was none of his business. He moved about the dance hall on catlike feet, seeing to it that the male customers danced every dance and bought drinks for themselves and their partners between dances. For many a year sightseers went to Harry Hill's just for a lark; as long as they paid, they were welcome.

John Allen's place was cut from another bolt. Located far down on Water Street, it combined the attributes of a concert saloon and a whorehouse. His girls served drinks, danced, and went upstairs with those men who sought their company. They wore the usual dance hall costume of tight bodice and short skirt but also wore tiny

Harry Hill's concert saloon on Houston Street, where high and low life me

bells on their red boots. Over and above the sound of the orchestra and the loud laughter of the half-drunken men one could hear the eerie tinkling of little bells as the girls went about their nightly chores.

Allen himself was a paradox. The son of a decent family, he had studied for the ministry at the Union Theological Seminary, but religion did not satisfy him and he went into the magdalen business in a fine private house that stood out like a sore thumb among the tenements and slums of the waterfront. As his profits increased, he became rougher and more uncouth, slapping the girls when they paused to rest, admitting young boys and girls in their early teens, and blinking at perversion. Yet all the while he kept a Bible on the bar, and sometimes read from it to visiting reformers to prove he was no worse than the bankers, railroad magnates, and promoters who were stealing from innocent investors. Like the Gideon Society in later years, he put a Bible in each of the bedrooms upstairs, convinced that the Good Book's physical presence somehow rectified all evil.

It was the clergy who finally ended Allen's skyrocketing climb to fame and riches. A group of them accepted his challenge one evening and held a prayer meeting in the concert saloon. A little later they rented the whole place for a handsome fee and held prayer meetings for a month. When Allen reopened, the old crowd did not come back, feeling he had made an obscene bargain, not with the devil, but with the forces of righteousness. It was a strange ending for the man whom several New York newspapers called the most evil man in the city.

Just as strange perhaps was the fact that the same newspapers considered Mme. Restell the most evil woman, a charge which bothered her not at all. Harry Hill and John Allen, and all the other proprietors of saloons and gambling dives, were objects of public obloquy because they promoted the high, wide, and open life that marked New York by night. Mme. Restell, on the contrary, was busy quietly and secretly rectifying mistakes that often resulted from attendance at such places. Many of the young women from the better houses of prostitution turned to the female "physician" when they found themselves pregnant. The abortionist, without actually taking part in the night life, knew what went on in town better than anyone else.

Among the surest sources of revenue for the lady at 160 Chambers Street were the houses of assignation. These establishments were scattered throughout the city, some consisting of small residential buildings, others of suites in some of the best hotels in town. Secrecy was their trademark. Unlike the saloons and bagnios, which advertised themselves with bright lights and colored posters, the assignation houses operated under the cloak of decorum and propriety.

The women who used these rooms were married women, very likely, and often of high station. Either deserted by their husbands or tired of their mates' lack of interest in them, they formed liaisons that required a safe meeting place. Seeking romance, these women and their lovers found secluded rooms and suites in midtown Manhattan. Sometimes they told their families they were going to the country, or to visit relatives, and hurried to their love nests. Their lovers of the moment would be given keys to the rooms. Assignation houses were operated by discreet landlords or hotel-keepers who knew exactly what was going on, but more timid, or wiser, some women set up their own ménages with the greatest circumspection.

For most of them it was a pathetic escape. They seldom found the lasting involvement of which most dreamed. Instead there was betrayal, suspicion, and often that meanest of crimes, blackmail. When, as often happened, these women found themselves pregnant and could not cozen their husbands into the role of cuckold, there was nothing for it but to turn to an abortionist. Mme. Restell, with her fame and steady advertising, got her fair share, or more, of the business.

Not all her customers were well-to-do, by any means. She cared for poor women along with the others, in what may have been her way of trying to provide justice. Maria Bodine was not her only poor patient. Mme. Restell delivered babies and induced miscarriages for servant girls, for wives and mothers who wanted no more children, and for immigrant women, and not solely for the daughters of the rich.

One day an immigrant woman not long in this country from Germany entered the Restell waiting room and asked the proprietor to care for her while she awaited the birth of her child. Her name was Frederica Medinger and she lived at 20 Stanton Street, hardly one of the better streets in town.

Months later—the year was 1855—the Medinger woman swore to a complaint charging Mme. Restell with kidnapping. According to the affidavit, the German immigrant had been admitted as a "roomer" at 160 Chambers Street and as the time of her accouchement approached she was given six pills by the abortionist. The Medinger woman swore that she was then delivered of a fine healthy baby. A day later when she asked to see her child, she was told it had disappeared.

Neither the newspapers nor court records reveal what happened to the infant, but it apparently met the same fate as Mary Applegate's: It had been "let out" for adoption. Events went forward mysteriously, and when the case was called for a hearing the Medinger woman did not show up in court. Several papers charged the abortionist with having bribed her way out of the law's toils. Obviously pressure had been brought to bear and somehow the whole incident was hushed up. No one ever heard of the woman or her baby again.

The newspapers repeated the charge that Mme. Restell was motivated solely by greed, and her actions often seemed to support the accusation. But a few persons wondered and came to believe that there might be a bit of the Robin Hood about the woman. Her persistence in caring for poor women in distress makes the supposition more than plausible. Mme. Restell left no diaries or letters to reveal her own inner thoughts, but it seems reasonable to suggest that she may well have seen the unfairness in the social life of a town where wealthy women could buy escape from shame while the poor could not. By lowering her rates for the less well-to-do she was, in her own way, squaring moral accounts.

"SERGEANT, DON'T MAKE ANY ARRESTS"

For Mme. Restell the outbreak of the Civil War meant one important thing: Her illicit career would be overlooked in the horror and anxieties of a fratricidal war. As long as the conflict lasted, she would exist more or less in a vacuum; the city authorities would be preoccupied with far more important problems.

Although she had served a year in prison, been charged with kidnapping or sequestering two infants, and accused of secretly causing the deaths of several women, Mme. Restell had come through her travail almost unscathed. She had improved her status and surroundings and undoubtedly fashioned a strong web of influence in high places.

Now that the nation was at war her unavoidable, perpetual fear of exposure could abate. Her crimes would shrink in importance. Who, when men were dying by the thousands on distant battlefields, would bother with Mme. Restell?

Through the streets of New York City marched men from New England and "York State" on their way to

southern towns most persons had never heard about.
Across the river in the Brooklyn Navy Yard a Swedish
inventor worked on a gunboat that would change the complexion of naval warfare. The finest families in town sent
their sons off to battle, some in blue, some in fancy National Guard uniforms, some in the exotic baggy trousers
and turbans of the Zouaves, patterned on a French regiment. On their heels followed a few women eager to join
Clara Barton in nursing the wounded.

After the second battle of Bull Run and Stonewall
Jackson's victories in the Shenandoah Valley, the bloom
was rubbed from the peach. Casualty lists grew longer
and the boasting that the Rebels would be whipped in a
few weeks sounded like a boy's words shouted into an
empty culvert. New York City settled down to the grim
business of fighting a hideous war.

The Democrats mustered their strength to end the war.
Meetings were held at which petitions were signed urging
Abraham Lincoln to seek an early peace. The Copperhead
conspiracy had its headquarters in this city where courage
and patriotism seemed overcome by pacifism and fear.

Fernando Wood, the fashion plate who held the reins
at City Hall, pleaded with the Common Council to secede
from the Union so that the city might support and sell
supplies to the Southern Confederacy.

Torn by dissension, frightened by rumors of revolt, its
parks and open squares turned into bivouacs for soldiers,
New York became a place where, in addition to factional
fury, many sought to forget the war in carnal pleasures.
Cock-pits opened, followed by rat-pits, where terriers
fought with vicious rats. The grog shops stayed open all
night, the waterfront dives lured soldiers and sailors to
depravity and death, and Greene Street was a roaring

carnival where the lights never dimmed—even in daylight.

Business boomed at 160 Chambers Street. Innocent girls who rode the steam trains from all over the northeast to say farewell to their sweethearts succumbed to the appeals of the men, as girls so often do on the eve of departures for war, and as a result of their ardor and indiscretion, Mme. Restell had all she could do to comply with frantic entreaties.

Her patients came on foot and in carriages. Some wore country clothes and some were dressed in satin. All had need of her services and all paid as much as they could. Charles Lohman, alias "Dr. Moreceau," and Joseph Trow hired new shipping clerks to mail their worthless nostrums across the land. Their bank accounts swelled and they opened fresh accounts. Mme. Restell herself was a depositor fawned upon by more than one churchgoing, psalm-singing banker whose reputation was like Caesar's wife's: above suspicion.

New York was growing fast, partly by immigration but mainly because it was one of the main shipping centers for war goods. The open fields north of 59th Street were now cluttered with shanties where laborers lived in squalor. The rugged hills of Central Park, on which work had begun in 1857 but was now at a standstill, swarmed with squatters, hungry children, and wandering goats, all living out a miserable existence.

Broadway and Eighth Avenue made a crossing at the southwestern corner of the land set aside for the great park. There were magnificent plans on Frederick Law Olmstead's drawing board for this open space to be publicly owned in the heart of Manhattan, but in the years when the Civil War marched to a climax at Gettysburg the scene was still rural. A great white barn stood almost where the avenues meet today and a fence surrounded a pigsty, paddock, and manure pile just across Broadway from where the Coliseum now rises above Columbus Circle.

The first two years of the war changed New York in a thousand ways, but not Mme. Restell. She was incredibly busy but could find little cause for complaint. She watched the army build wooden barracks all along the eastern side of City Hall Park to house transient soldiers, but that invasion hardly affected her. The guests at the swank Astor House didn't like the change in their view but P. T. Barnum was delighted to see all this activity. It brought many more persons within easy access of his museum and showhouse, and they were the sort of people who would spend a quarter for admission—something the swells of the Astor House seldom did.

When she went out occasionally—she made her own deposits in her several savings banks—Mme. Restell noted with disgust that the streets were in poor shape: unswept and full of potholes. This situation was the result of a standoff in the city government. Fernando Wood had been beaten after his second term as mayor, and George Opdyke, a Republican, took office in 1862. Anything Opdyke wanted, the Democrats in the council defeated. It was a wonder water still flowed from the Croton system.

This was the situation when Congress established the pattern for a draft by passing the Conscription Act in March 1863. The bloody battles in Virginia and along the Mississippi threatened to leave the Union Army depleted; only a universal draft could refill the ranks.

To New York, the idea of conscription was anathema. At least a fourth of the population was Irish, most of them recent arrivals driven from their homes by the potato famines. In no time at all these immigrants were saying they had not come to America to free the slaves.

The governor, Horatio Seymour, was an outspoken Democrat, violently opposed to the war and the draft. "Boss" Bill Tweed, who ruled the Democratic machine in New York, also wanted neither. Mass meetings were organized all over town to protest the war's continuation. Some who attended were important, decent men. Others were riffraff from the docks and slums.

On July 11, the first names in the city were drawn for conscription from a rotating drum, and there was no disturbance. But on the second day, July 13, a Monday, the opponents of the draft were ready. They massed by the hundreds on Sixth Avenue, marched uptown, gathering forces from stores and factories along the way, turned east and tore down the telegraph wires along the New York and Harlem Railway, and then attacked the enrollment office at 46th Street and Third Avenue.

There can be no question but that this mob movement was well organized. By noon the city was in panic: Policemen were being chased and beaten or murdered, and forty men of the Army's Invalid Corps, summoned in desperation, were beaten with their own muskets and stabbed with their own bayonets. Police Superintendent John Kennedy —he who had told the clergy and reformers that New York was not truly an evil place—was beaten nearly to death.

By noon terror was abroad throughout the city. Tracks were torn up on two railroads, several blocks of residences were in flames, and an estimated 50,000 rioters ran loose on Third Avenue from Cooper Union to the East Forties. A regiment of marines hurried across from the Navy Yard to protect the Custom House. An appeal for federal troops went out to the forts guarding the harbor. In the afternoon two armed warships took up stations, one in the

Hudson, one in the East River, their guns aimed to protect the buildings of the financial district.

At an undetermined hour shortly after noon the rampaging mobs ceased fighting the police and started attacking blacks—men, women, and children. Hunting them out in the shabbier warrens of the town, the rioters beat, stabbed, and killed them as if in sport. Then, shouting and cursing, they headed for the Colored Orphan Asylum, a large building on Fifth Avenue between 43rd and 44th streets. With but minutes to spare the superintendent ushered the frightened children out of a rear door and into the street where they scurried to safety while the mob beat down the front doors. Angry to find no children, the rioters set fire to the orphanage and stoned the firemen who tried to put out the blaze.

Mayor Opdyke telegraphed Washington for troops, urging that New York regiments resting after the Union victory at Gettysburg be hurried to save their hometown. But the troops were far away and the temper of the mob was growing worse by the minute. Private houses were broken into, ostensibly for the purpose of tracking down fleeing blacks. If any blacks were found, those whites who had offered them a haven were beaten or killed. If no blacks were unearthed, jewels were stolen, people roughly handled, and the houses were often set afire.

Most of the heavy fighting between the outnumbered police and the rioters took place above Canal Street, but Mme. Restell, with her servants and the frightened patients, could hear the sharp crack of musketry, an occasional boom of howitzers brought by ferry from Governor's Island, and the jangling bells of horse-drawn fire engines. A dense pall of smoke hung over the hot, terrified city.

Then those in the Restell house heard a new outbreak

The destruction of the Colored Orphan Asylum.

THE BRUTAL MURDER OF COLONEL O'BRIEN BY THE RIOTERS IN FORTY-SIXTH STREET.

Another casualty of the Civil War draft riots.

of firing and shouting, this time much nearer. They knew nothing of the latest violence except that it was far too close to where they cowered in their shuttered house. What had happened was this: Officials acting in place of the wounded Superintendent Kennedy heard that a new mob was heading down Broadway to assault police head-quarters and City Hall. Thomas C. Acton, commissioner of police, who was trying to fill Kennedy's shoes, called Sergeant Daniel Carpenter to his desk. The officer was told to take 200 men, almost all of the reserves that had not been injured, and ordered not to wait for the on-coming mob but to march north and meet it. "Sergeant," added the police commissioner, "don't make any arrests."

Carpenter led his valiant group up Broadway, met the rioters, and fought them to a standstill with billies and revolvers. Heads were cracked and policemen went down under a rain of paving blocks; but after an hour the rioters fled the scene, leaving many a desperately wounded or dead companion behind.

Nightfall, for which every decent person prayed hoping it would curb the violence, brought even greater terror to those hiding behind barred doors and windows at 160 Chambers Street. A mob numbering several thousand gathered west of Broadway not far from the Restell establishment, then stormed across City Hall Park hoping to ransack the lower floors of the *Tribune* building on Park Row. Horace Greeley's support of the war was well known and the mob sought "retribution."

From the decimated ranks of the police precincts in lower Manhattan a force of patrolmen was formed and joined by soldiers from Governor's Island. With quiet resolution they charged the mob tearing at the newspaper office, beat the rioters with nightsticks and rifle butts, and drove them away from the district by midnight. As his-

Mobs stormed the Tribune *building on Park Row seeking retribution for publisher Horace Greeley's support of the war.*

tories tell us only of large events, no one can tell what relief must have been felt by the frightened people in the Restell house when quiet at last descended on Manhattan.

But the draft riots were far from over. The next morning, Tuesday the fourteenth, those inhabitants who had managed to sleep awoke to find the streets a shambles. Omnibuses had been turned over and burned or had fled to distant carbarns. Banks, stores, factories, and other businesses were closed, their employees gathered inside, armed with ancient muskets, squirrel guns, heavy sticks, and rocks gathered from the torn-up pavements outside.

The mayor had pleaded with Governor Seymour to come down from Albany to quiet the mob, but the Democratic politician hesitated until much later on that second day of rioting. For the time, at least, the fate of the city was in the hands of Opdyke, Acton, and a few thousand policemen of incredible courage. Fighting broke out early on Second Avenue, with bluecoats and soldiers fighting the rioters hand to hand on rooftops. There was no quarter given: The weaker man was thrown to the street below.

Then the mob learned that a supply of arms was stored in the factory of the Union Steam Works near Second Avenue and 21st Street. Forty policemen stood guard inside. Here the battle raged for hours until the police, most of them struck by flying rocks, had to retreat, using a small opening in the rear wall and running across a stonemason's yard. The mob rushed inside, gloating in victory. As they started to gather up the arms the stairway collapsed. Then fire broke out and scores of the rioters died in the flames.

On Wednesday and again on Thursday morning the rioting continued, but the mob spirit had been broken by the unflinching courage of the police. Thousands of decent citizens had fled to Westchester, Brooklyn, and New Jersey, some paying scandalous fees for a ride behind speeding horses. Brooklyn, then a separate city, sent a thousand uniformed policemen across on the ferries to aid their exhausted mates on the New York force.

By midday of Thursday the tide turned. Five regiments of army regulars arrived by train from Washington, crossed the Hudson, and took up positions in key parts of the city. Working with the policemen now relieved to see new forces of law and order at their side, the soldiers began clearing the streets. By the time the church clocks chimed midnight the city was under control again. Even the toughest of thugs and bullies wanted no part of a battle with soldiers who had stood up to Lee's armies. The next day eight more regiments reached New York and all danger was past. More than 1200 persons had been killed in four days of carnage and arson. How many others were wounded was never determined. The city spent millions to repair the damage.

Mme. Restell could count herself fortunate. Her house was undamaged, her staff intact, and not one of her patients harmed.

RED LIGHTS SHINING
ALL OVER TOWN

Victory for the Union brought the city an era of good times. The depression of 1857 had been swept into oblivion by the war, and peace found everyone eager to get rich, seek new fortunes in the west, or at least have a good time right at home.

As in every postwar society, morals suffered. Soldiers came home to new conditions, new careers, and new lives free of the perpetual fear of death or wounds and rejoiced in being alive. Greene Street, which had boomed during the four years of conflict, rose to still noisier and more debased notoriety. Newspapers which had devoted columns to lists of the dead and wounded now used their type to sell sex in a dozen different forms. The lists of "personals" grew longer and longer. Some mentioned "quiet room to let with board for lady only" which any ninny could interpret as a place of assignation. Others advertised saloons for the very young, or the physical attractions of certain dancers to be seen nightly at East Side halls.

Then a new type of "personal" began to appear in the

papers. Couched in clever ambiguities, nonetheless they
were open offers to meet members of the other sex, often
persons whom they had encountered perhaps in the horsecars, or at the theater, or in a store.

James D. McCabe, Jr., who was a minister as well as
a crime reporter, compiled a book in 1872 on the good
and evil faces of New York. He cites there some of these
notices from the daily papers:

> Tall Lady dressed in black, who
> acknowledged gentleman's salute,
> Broadway and Tenth street. Please
> address D, Box 119————office, if
> she wishes to form his acquaintance.

> Lady in Grand Street Car, Saturday
> evening 7:30.—Had on plaid shawl,
> black silk dress; noticed gentleman
> in front; both got out at the Bowery;
> will oblige by sending her address to
> C. L. Box 199————office.

> Miss Gertie Davis, formerly of Lex-
> ington Avenue, will be pleased to see
> her friends at 106 Clinton Place.

The dozens of such readily understood notices amounted
to a modern forum where the public was told how to ar-
range illicit meetings, what new faces were to be found
among the waiter-girls in the concert saloons, or where
prostitutes now lived after moving from one house of ill
fame to another. Their male friends must not be allowed
to wonder where they were.

Paradoxically, the number of streetwalkers in the city
increased rather than decreased after the war. Peace usually brings the opposite situation. Whether this was the

result of the South's defeat and the cruel handling of Reconstruction by the carpetbaggers is beyond establishing, but at the time some students of social history believed the phenomenon stemmed from those reasons. One of these observers was a prominent New Yorker and man-about-town named George Templeton Strong. Of excellent family, he served on boards of directors of banks and business firms, was appointed to various civic organizations, and otherwise moved in the most elegant circles in town. In spite of these many obligations, he kept a diary. Near the end of the war—it was in an entry dated November 26, 1864—Strong hints that the increase in prostitution did arise from the discomfiture of the South:

> George Anthon dined here and spent the evening. He tells me that according to the talk of the New York Club the harlotry of the city is largely reinforced by Southern refugee women who were of good social standing at home but find themselves here without means of support and forced to choose between starving and whoring. . . . It seems a just retribution of the Southern slaveholding chivalry who have been forcing their female slaves—black, mulatto, and quadroon—to minister to their pleasures that their rebellion should drive their wives and daughters to flee northward and prostitute themselves to Northern "mudsills" and plebeian "Yankees." All the North is full of these refugees, male and female. One of them tried to seduce Burnside the other day in Washington and nearly succeeded, but as she was turning down the gas he remembered Molly [Mrs. Burnside] and fled the room.

Strong, McCabe, and other writers of the period agreed that the city was infested with streetwalkers—whatever the cause. They were most common on Broadway, but also frequented Third, Fourth, and Sixth Avenues. Fifth Avenue sported a few, but the police, aware of the wishes of the genteel folk whose residences lined that thoroughfare, discouraged solicitation on that privileged street.

As soon as darkness fell the prostitutes appeared—old, young, even girls in their teens—some rather pretty, but most of them painted in a futile attempt to disguise their

NEW-YORK *by* GAS-LIGHT.

Hooking a Victim.

*"Hooking a Victim" was a common occurrence
on the streets of old New York.*

109

plainness or the ravages of sin. They walked "at a rapid pace peculiar to them," one observer said, glancing at all the men they passed and whispering to them in a guarded undertone. The police kept the women from soliciting at length on the avenues, but if a girl succeeded in interesting a man there, they both stepped into a side street to complete the arrangement, free from interference from the patrolmen.

All over the main downtown section of Manhattan were the cheap lodging houses where the streetwalkers rented rooms by the week. If a man accepted a girl's offer she would lead him to her room in one of these "bed houses," as they were called. If he was lucky he left unharmed, although venereal disease was rampant among the lost sisterhood. If he was not lucky he would discover—later —that the streetwalker had a male accomplice, known to the police as a panel thief. Between them the two had everything prepared for the victim's reception.

Panel thieves worked cleverly. At one end of the prostitute's room they built a partition papered over in the same design as that of the room, but in this false wall was a sliding panel which could be moved silently. The only furniture in a room in a bed house was a bed, a chair, and a ceiling lamp. The girl saw to it that the chair was always placed close to the sliding panel. When the man who had been picked up or "hooked," as the phrase went, entered the room, he put his clothes in the only logical place: the chair. While he was pleasantly engaged, her accomplice behind the false wall slid the panel back, reached through, and stole the money from the gay blade's wallet, usually leaving a few dollar bills. The girl, knowing what would happen, had insisted upon being paid in advance; the man would therefore dress and leave, unaware that he had been robbed.

Most men victimized by panel thieves never reported the theft, preferring to take their loss and avoid publicity. The few who went to the local precinct house to enter a complaint were scoffed at. Or if the police did go back to the room with the complainant both girl and accomplice were gone, not to return until "the law" had left.

A few of the streetwalkers also worked hand in glove with more evil characters. When unsuspecting men accompanied the prostitute to her place, he found it somewhat better furnished, in fact not unlike that in a working-class tenement. After the customer had taken off his clothes the sliding panel would open and a man appeared, charging his "wife" with being untrue and demanding a large sum to keep from lodging a complaint and having the "adulterer" arrested. This old "badger game," or "husband game," netted the criminals more money, but the police who laughed at the panel thieves worked diligently to discourage the other ploy, which was blackmail. They knew that such criminals usually turned to violence and even murder if the victim refused to pay or had too thin a wallet to please the "husband."

The decent inhabitants of New York disliked the notoriety the city earned from newspaper exposés and from the crusades of clergymen eager to retrieve the reputation of this scond Sodom. A few citizens banded together to establish missions where prostitutes were invited to come in and be saved.

The year after Lee surrendered to Grant at Appomattox Court House a group of these citizens, most of them churchwomen, formed the Midnight Mission as a refuge for prostitutes. They were brave people, these reformers, and they located their mission at 260 Greene Stret, right in the middle of the worst sin street in town.

Most of the inmates of the houses, and the streetwalkers

who could not get employment in the better brothels, jeered at the women who staffed the mission, but a few accepted invitations to enter and be redeemed. The prim little cards handed to the girls by the mission workers bore this message:

> *The Committee of the Midnight Mission*
> *will be happy to see you at tea*
> *on Friday evening, at 10 P.M.*
> *at No. 260 Greene Street.*

> ———

> ROOMS OPEN EVERY DAY FROM 2:00 TO 4:00 P.M.
> FOR PRIVATE CONVERSATION AND FRIENDLY
> ADVICE.

Many of these invitations were tossed into the gutter, but some of the recipients stopped in to see if, after all, there was some way out of their miserable life. Statistics compiled by another nonsectarian mission, the Magdalen Society, showed what had been accomplished in thirty-five years. During this period the Magdalen Society housed 2,000 inmates at one time or another, of whom 600 were placed with private families, 400 restored to relatives, 400 left the mission at their own request, 300 ducked out without permission, probably to go back to their old lives, 300 were transferred to hospitals, 41 died, 20 married, and 24 were received into evangelical churches, obviously saved from wickedness.

While sin and righteousness battled over these poor creatures, Mme. Restell reaped her illicit harvest year after year. She ended pregnancies for the younger inmates of brothels and rescued the ennui-ridden women who had dallied unluckily in houses of assignation.

But these were not the only profits that found their way to 160 Chambers Street. Venereal disease afflicted many

112

of both sexes. There was no known cure that was infallible, but quack physicians thrived on dosing panic-stricken patients. It was a situation made to order for Charles Lohman and his bother-in-law. Advertisements in all the newspapers sufficed to trap new victims eager to pay for nonexistent medicines that never cured.

If foreigners thought New York a second Sodom, the residents knew better. Trouble, crime, and self-indulgence were everywhere, but people were so busy making a living, building a new city, and recovering from the war that thousands had no time for sin even if they had had the wish and the wherewithal. Because the island of Manhattan is much longer than it is wide, most men had to travel a considerable distance from home to office. Morning and evening they rode the horse-drawn streetcars down the avenues to the financial and trading centers from uptown houses around Washington Square, Murray Hill, or Chelsea.

John Stephenson built most of these vehicles, commonly known as stages, in a plant on 27th Street between Madison and Fourth Avenues, a region then considered rather far out in the country. Stephenson put New York on wheels until the railroads took over the chore. His coaches were gay splashes of color which shone even more resplendently because the buildings along the streets were dully alike and uninspired in material and design.

The earlier horsecars held about twenty persons, but later when they ran on iron rails they carried many more. In the 1860s as now the cars were crowded during rush hours, and young men and boys hung on the steps and sides like monkeys in a tree. A French observer went back to Paris and told a scandalous lie that was printed in a picture paper, to the horror of Americans there and here. Young ladies wishing to ride the horsecars, even when they were full, he said, were in the habit of getting aboard and sitting on the laps of men already seated.

Stephenson built a score or so of "Special" cars which were masterpieces of the wagonmaker's art. They had swinging overhead lights that burned coal oil, banquettes and movable armchairs upholstered in plush and velvet, and floors carpeted from wall to wall. Riders of these deluxe cars paid an extra fare for the privilege, but often rowdies jumped aboard, offering only the regular payment. Sometimes the conductors would push them off, but at other times, afraid that the public would raise a cry about undemocratic behavior, the traction company owners directed the conductors to let such men ride without extra fare. The "common people" were already asserting their strength.

Brooks Brothers' store had been gutted and ravaged during the draft riots and had to be rebuilt. A. T. Stewart, the city's first big mercantile tycoon, was luckier. His store, on Broadway between Chambers and Reade in the block just above City Hall Park, had escaped damage because of its nearness to the seat of government.

But as postwar business boomed, Stewart felt the need of larger quarters and moved many blocks up Broadway to 10th Street. Other stores began eyeing locations near Grand and Houston Streets, and the center of the shopping district gravitated steadily northward. This discommoded many customers; it also bothered the old apple woman. For years she had sat in a chair on the sidewalk beside the main entrance to Stewart's emporium. When he moved to fancier quarters in the world's largest mercantile building, the old lady hesitated to follow. In a gesture that might have been inspired by one of Madison Avenue's top public relations counselors a hundred years later, Stewart had the chair moved to a new place of

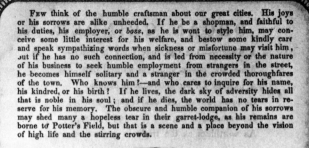

Few think of the humble craftsman about our great cities. His joys or his sorrows are alike unheeded. If he be a shopman, and faithful to his duties, his employer, or *boss*, as he is wont to style him, may conceive some little interest for his welfare, and bestow some kindly care and speak sympathizing words when sickness or misfortune may visit him, but if he has no such connection, and is led from necessity or the nature of his business to seek humble employment from strangers in the street, he becomes himself solitary and a stranger in the crowded thoroughfares of the town. Who knows him?—and who cares to inquire for his name, his kindred, or his birth? If he lives, the dark sky of adversity hides all that is noble in his soul; and if he dies, the world has no tears in reserve for his memory. The obscure and humble companion of his sorrows may shed many a hopeless tear in their garret-lodge, as his remains are borne to Potter's Field, but that is a scene and a place beyond the vision of high life and the stirring crowds.

OLD APPLE WOMAN AT STEWART'S.

Our Young Readers may some of them have seen the aged woman sitting in an old-fashioned board chair, at the front of Stewart's new dry-goods temple, in Broadway. A little basket of apples, from which she retails to the visitors of that establishment, exonerates her from the charge of vagrancy, and gives her something of the credit and character of a respectable and regular business. We know nothing of her position or history, beyond what is expressed below. An incident has been related in the newspapers, that speaks well for her character, as well as for the goodness of the enterprising merchant through whose indulgence she has been afforded an opportunity to pursue her occupation.

When Mr. Stewart removed from his old store to his present splendid establishment, the old apple woman was much troubled that her stand had become worthless, and she dare not obtrude on the steps of the new temple.

When A. T. Stewart moved his shop to larger quarters, he transported the old apple woman's chair to its new place of honor, right by the front door.

honor, right by his front door. It made the old apple woman very happy and warmed the hearts of thousands of New Yorkers.

The movement uptown grew apace. The mansions that had seemed so well situated in the region of present-day Washington Square, Greenwich Village, and Lafayette Street became a little dowdy in their owners' eyes. The Astors moved up to Fifth Avenue near 34th and 35th Streets and Mr. Stewart, his dry goods palace still thriving, built a fine mansion on Fifth Avenue across the street from where the Empire State Building now sends its lofty spire into the sky.

None of these signs of change escaped the sharp eye of Mme. Restell. When Stewart moved his store away from *her* street, she realized that forces were afoot that would alter the entire complexion of the city. The construction of Saint Patrick's Cathedral at Fifth Avenue and 50th Street, under way since 1860 after long wartime interruptions, was nearing completion. Columbia College, which, from the days of English rule until a few years before, had existed just a few blocks from her establishment, was now in session a block or so away from the new cathedral.

If the richest families in town, the new Catholic cathedral, the city's largest and oldest institution of higher learning, and many another body all felt the urge to move uptown, what was there to stop Mme. Restell, also an institution as the great and successful abortionist, from following suit? She talked the move over with her husband, and as he usually did, he agreed wholeheartedly. They would not only leave lower Manhattan but would build a house that could stand comparison with just about any other residence in the whole town.

The female "physician" ordered up her carriage and

drove northward to pick a site. It was not easy. Here and there north of 42nd Street new structures were going up, some of them fine mansions. But in between there was still open ground where goats foraged or truck farming went on. Mme. Restell made several trips away from home before she decided on a suitable spot.

She chose a lot on Fifth Avenue, right in the midst of some of the newest and fanciest town houses in the city. On the northeast corner of 52nd Street she sat in her carriage, obviously well satisfied with herself, as a surveyor drove stakes into the earth establishing the boundaries of her future home. She was a canny, prudent woman, however, and was careful to hold her parasol in such a way that passersby could not recognize her. She wanted the house finished—a *fait accompli*—before the residents nearby knew who their new neighbor was.

THE SINISTER HOUSE
ON FIFTH AVENUE

An occasional story was printed in the papers about the Restell mansion as it was being built and after she moved in. These differed in many ways, as many as the descriptions they gave of the interior of the house. Reportage was far less careful than it is today, not only because litigation is more common now and damages much higher, but because writers for the daily press neglected to check their facts.

One of the papers carried an article stating that Mme. Restell bought the house already finished through a real estate agent. It was hinted that otherwise no one would have sold a house in that location to such a notorious woman. Other papers seemed sure she had built it herself, which is much more probable, and that she decorated it herself. Here again the press could not agree. Some papers said she used garish and even ugly furnishings, while others were just as sure that the decor was tasteful. Readers must have wondered at the varied descriptions, but had they known that almost no one had been inside the building they would have understood the variations.

Residence of Charles R. Luhman.

The house at 657 Fifth Avenue where Madame Restell ended her life.

The house was of brownstone, four stories high, with a basement whose windows were almost above street level. From the lower floors it was easy to look up and down Fifth Avenue for blocks because of the vacant lots in the neighborhood. From upper stories the abortionist could see Central Park to the north.

One writer said the house was furnished like a palace. There were fifty-two windows, each made up of two immense panes of glass. They were hung with satin and French lace curtains, which another tyro historian claimed were extremely vulgar.

119

The female "physician" established her office in a basement room, which despite its location was light and airy.
Here her callers conferred with her and made arrangements for their needs. There is no better way to describe
the rest of the mansion than to use the words James
McCabe used in 1872, but as he said he was quoting from
another, the authorship cannot be established:

> On the first floor are the grand hall of tessellated
> marble, lined with mirrors; the three immense
> dining-rooms, [just why there were so many
> seemed unimportant to McCabe] furnished in
> bronze and gold, with yellow satin hangings, an
> enormous French mirror in mosaic gilding at every
> panel; ceilings in medalions [sic] and cornices;
> more parlors and reception-rooms; butler's pan-
> try, lined with solid silver services; dining room
> with all imported furniture. Other parlors on the
> floor above; a guest-chamber in blue brocade satin,
> with gold- and-ebony bedstead elegantly covered;
> boudoir for dressing in every room, madam and
> husband's own room, granddaughter's room, news-
> room, study. Fourth floor—servant's rooms in
> mahogany and Brussels carpet, and circular
> picture-gallery; the fifth floor contains a magnifi-
> cent billiard room, dancing-hall, with pictures,
> piano, etc., and commands a fine view of Fifth
> Avenue. The whole house is filled with statuettes,
> paintings, rare bronzes, ornamental and valuable
> clocks, candelabras, silver globes and articles of
> many origins and rare worth.

But if there was disagreement as to the interior decor
of the mansion, it was nothing to the divergence in facts
dealing with the owner's own family. It was generally believed that she had two daughters before she married

Charles Lohman. Some gossips said she was on friendly terms with both yet insisted on their living far out of the city so that they would not be affected in their reputations by their mother's activities. Another version had it that one of the daughters had a daughter of her own by a policeman with whom she ran away. It was supposedly this child for whom the bedroom cited by McCabe was furnished in the Fifth Avenue mansion. Those who believed this story also claimed to know that the other daughter never married, despite an offer by her mother to settle a quarter of a million dollars on anyone claiming her hand in marriage.

One of the pamphleteers who got into print as fast as type could be set after Mme. Restell died included a touching anecdote to show that, evil though she was, she loved her own children and grandchildren. This writer said she commissioned a well-known Italian sculptor to design a tombstone for a small grandchild's grave and held a dead infant on a quilt on her lap for the artist to see just how she wanted the finished effigy to appear.

According to this same writer, a verse was graven on the granite marker, bearing these lines:

> *Hush, tread lightly, our child is sleeping;*
> *Her life on earth is o'er;*
> *Vacant hearts at home are weeping,*
> *She sleeps to wake no more.*

Whatever the truth of these statements about the abortionist, it is clear that the house was built about the time John Roebling started erecting the Brooklyn Bridge in 1870. A few months before a group known as the Société des Bals d'Artistes staged a masked ball at the French Theater on Fourteenth Street—a riotous, risqué affair which set tongues to wagging all over town. While this was being talked about, very little attention was given to the building of another rich man's mansion on Fifth Avenue.

The *World* asserted that the Société organized the masked ball only to make money and to afford an opportunity for a good deal of French carousing. The newspaper was unable to state whether the first goal was achieved, but its many columns of description left no doubt that the second was attained.

The covering of news has changed but little over the decades. Then, as with some papers even today, nothing pleased the editors more than to write as explicitly as they could about sin and crime, all the while uttering sanctimonious disapproval. After describing the arrival of the costumed and masked guests who were greeted outside by rowdy men freely making impertinent comments, one paper went on to say that most of the women wore clothes that exposed as much of their persons as possible. Many were attired in short ballet skirts; others wore trunk hose and fleshings, or tried to emulate the garb of Hindustani *bayadères*, or, again, naughty "daughters of the regiment."

Then the paper becomes more specific:

> One of the women has been caught up by the crowd and tossed bodily into the proscenium box, where she is caught and dragged by half a dozen brutes in over the sill and furniture in such a manner as to disarrange as much as possible what small vestige of raiment there is on her. . . . Presently the trick is repeated on the other side. A young woman, rather pretty and dressed in long skirts, is thrown up, and falls back into the arms

of the crowd, who turn her over, envelop her head in her own skirts, and again toss her up temporarily denuded.

Later on in this article the writer, now carried away by his own words, is moved to even more moralistic description:

> There is not a whisper of shame in the crowd. It is now drunken with liquor and its own beastliness. It whirls in mad eddies round and round; the panting women in the delirium of excitement; their eyes, flashing with the sudden abnormal light of physical elation, bound and leap like tigresses; they have lost the last sense of prudence and safety. Some of them are unmasked, and reveal the faces of brazen and notorious she-devils.

If we can believe the *World* reporter, it was nothing short of a hairbreadth rescue of countless souls when at two o'clock in the morning the orchestra finally played "Home, Sweet Home."

Just ten years before the antics at the masked ball, the Prince of Wales, who later became King Edward VII, was feted by New York's most gilt-edged society and the administration. He was wined and dined at a cost estimated to be $750,000, but not one lady was tossed into the air, skirts over her head. The war years, everybody said, had eroded the moral fiber of New York City.

Yet all was not lost. About the same time that Mme. Restell could have been reading of these gay doings and discussing drapes and carpets with interior decorators, a new wing of St. Luke's Hospital was opened at the southwest corner of Fifth Avenue and 55th Street, three blocks from the abortionist's home. And the cornerstone of the Fifth Avenue Presbyterian Church was also being laid at the opposite corner from the hospital addition.

At last the Restell mansion was completed and the "most evil woman in the city" moved in, with seven servants in the house and four fast horses and a fine carriage in the stables in back. If anyone in the neighborhood was still ignorant as to who their new neighbor was, they soon found out. She did not waste any time admiring her satin curtains or her medallion-covered ceilings. Within a few nights of the move, muffled women were arriving at the side entrance on 52nd Street and scurrying inside. Quite naturally some of the residents were horrified. The owners of the vacant lots adjoining the Restell mansion could not sell them at any price. There were no takers. Some of the men got together for secret conferences and agreed to try to buy the woman "physician" out, but she laughed in their faces when they called on her with the proposition. "I did not buy the house for speculation," she is reported to have said. "I bought it as a home and I intend to remain in it as long as I live."

A short time later Charles Lohman died. It was a pity. The ex-printer had come a long way from the *Herald*'s crowded, dirty composing room and as "Dr. Moreceau" had grown to like the amenities of life that came with a steady and handsome income. But with this same move from Chambers Street to Fifth Avenue goes a minor mystery: Nothing more was heard of Joseph Trow. Whether he died before his brother-in-law or left the family business is not known. At any rate, Mme. Restell was left a widow, brotherless, and alone in the huge place except for her staff.

There were probably fewer than a score of women in New York who could boast of greater wealth than the abortionist. She could easily have retired and led a genteel, if somewhat isolated, social life. Although many of her patients came from the highest walks of life, they had nothing to do with her once their troubles were over. Perhaps it was just this that kept the woman in the big house at work. What else could she have done? She had thousands in the bank, one of the best houses in town, and few she could call a friend. Even the gaily decorated room furnished for her granddaughter went unoccupied.

Her one relaxation—or the only one that the public knew about—was to go for a drive every afternoon when the weather permitted. In summer her carriage was a familiar sight on the roads of Central Park—like those of the Astors, Morgans, Van Rensselaers, and other swells. In winter she bundled up in ermine lap robes and went sleighing "in tandem," her fleet-footed steeds stepping out with the best in town. Many another expensively dressed woman glanced covertly at the abortionist, but the men stared ahead, never lifting their toppers.

It is a tradition the world over to clothe certain houses with mystery, whether deserved or not. Mme. Restell's merited that aura. Whispered stories of hearses occasionally drawn up at the side door encouraged speculation. Years before, when the little frame house on Greenwich Street was the scene of the abortionist's activity, the mob had yelled to have the cellar floor dug up, convinced it was a charnel house filled with little skeletons. Rumors like these seldom die, and the people who walked past the corner of 52nd and Fifth did so with an ill-assured glance, as boys do when passing a graveyard in the dark. The sight of heavily veiled women entering and leaving did nothing to lighten the scene. Architecturally attractive, well-kept, and imposing, the corner house remained a center of suspicion.

IN THE WINGS;
A CRUSADER APPEARS

New York City at the time the elegant mansion was finished and Mme. Restell moved in was caught up in the throes of social change. In the late 1860s and early 1870s the expanding metropolis had fallen apart at the seams, mainly because of the Civil War and its effects. From Greene Street to the waterfront dives, from the fancy dress romps to the concert hall saloons, crime and sin rode double harness. Politics was as rotten as a badly spoiled melon. For many, graft was a way of life. For some a lack of decent laws made it easy for unscrupulous men to prey upon the poor, the hungry, and the weak. For still others the hectic rush for profits and pleasure blinded men and women who otherwise might have looked with greater charity and human kindness upon their less fortunate neighbors.

Yet although the gang fights and riots had subsided and relative calm had settled over the city—perhaps even because of this apparent fashioning of a lid of respectability over the sinful broth that bubbled below the surface —change was on the horizon. It had resulted earlier in the activities of such groups as the Midnight Mission and the Magdalen Society, in sermons from some of the pulpits, and in the revulsion that later led to the smashing of the Tweed Ring. Papers were full of news about new railroads, new ship lines, the rush to take up free land for homesteading in the West—in short with all the facets of expansion that had been held in check by the war and now shook the country to its very roots. It did not seem as though there was time or inclination for social change, but underneath all the exciting evidence of growth there was a force loose in the city which was growing in power— a manifestation of desire on the part of decent people for better conditions. Unknown to those like Mme. Restell, the owners of bagnios, and the operators of the evil rendezvous who had seemed so strongly entrenched during and just after the war, this force would destroy many of the more notable criminals and evildoers.

In fact, New York City at this time was made to order for reformers. One of the most famous of these was Anthony Comstock and he had already made a small reputation for himself. But Mme. Restell, now seemingly secure in her fine new home, her secrets a powerful weapon that appeared to give her considerable immunity from the law, did not suspect that her nemesis had already appeared in the wings. He was to spearhead the attack to be launched by reform elements against crime and sin. They did not know it, but the wicked of the city would have to deal with this man. To understand him better, it is necessary to go back and trace his beginnings.

The one person the abortionist would be unable to outwit was born on a hill farm in New Canaan, Connecticut, on March 7, 1844—years after the "female physician" was well established. His parents were of colonial stock and if ever a human being had the characteristics of an

The reforming zeal of Anthony Comstock destroyed Madame Restell, but he too had his critics, for example the artist who drew this cartoon satirizing Comstock's crusade against the Art Students' League.

English pit bulldog, it was this Yankee from the Nut-meg State.

Anthony's father was a well-intentioned man, over-whelmed by a brood of ten children, two sawmills, and a large farm. His mother was the dynamo of the family, a religious martinet who taught her children that hell's fire was just a step away for the sinner. It was she who in-sisted on hitching up the sleigh, even in severe winter storms, to get to the Congregational meetinghouse several miles away, and if every able-bodied member of the family had to get out and shovel away the snowdrifts, she thought it no more than right to suffer on the way to hear God's word.

To many of the parishioners the word *suffer* was en-tirely accurate. The morning service was long, with a ser-mon that seemed interminable. Immediately after came Sunday school, then a cold lunch eaten in the stables be-hind the church, and finally an afternoon prayer meeting. Chilled to the bone, the Comstocks returned home to share a small tea before going back again for an evening service.

From everything Anthony later wrote, we infer that he enjoyed every minute of the Sabbath and never minded the daily morning prayers and Bible reading around the dining room table. The boy never showed any inclination to enter the ministry, but he delighted in hearing how the wicked would be punished and how life was really little more than a rocky, arduous path that had to be endured in order to reach the bliss promised by Puritan preachers.

In his late teens the boy got a clerking job in Winni-pauk, working long hours and never complaining. One day children came running into the grocery store crying, "Mad dog! Mad dog!" Anthony went up to his room, got his muzzle-loading pistol, and went out to protect the community from the animal. But despite the crisis there was a short delay: It would not do to venture forth unprepared; Anthony got down on his knees and asked for divine help. Then he stepped into the dusty road and shot the mad dog straight through the head.

He performed this act of heroism when he was eighteen years old. When he was a year older he wrote in his diary that he would welcome the tomb if it were not for those left mourning behind him. He noted in the same diary that he "attended pr. meeting yet found no relief; instead each prayer or hymn seemed to add to my misery." Once, several years earlier, he had visited a neighbor despite parental orders to the contrary, and had shared a bottle of homemade wine with a boy of his own age. Giddy and exhilarated, he arrived home in a state of shame, and the licking he received behind the woodshed was welcomed rather than avoided. After all, he knew, sin was always punished. Anthony never took another drink in his life, by his own account, but the dangers of alcohol left an impression never to be erased.

Several months after slaying the rabid dog young Comstock found his hatred for strong spirits affronted by none other than the owner of the dead animal. This man was probably no more dissolute than any other saloon keeper of the time, but when the suggestion was made that he would accept groceries in lieu of cash against purchases of liquor, Anthony decided it was time for action. He asked the sheriff to aid him in closing the tavern, but the sheriff had his own reasons for declining. Young Comstock then formed a one-man vigilante committee, stole through the night to the saloon, and broke in. He had a holiday inside, opening the taps and bungs of beer kegs and smashing whiskey bottles. As the spirits ran onto the floor Anthony penned a note warning that if the publican reopened for business the building would be torn down board by board ad shingle by shingle.

The tavern keeper had an Achilles' heel: He was running the den of iniquity without a license. Having tasted the young crusader's venom, he decided it would be wiser to get out of town and open up elsewhere. Without further remonstrance, he slunk out of Winnipauk and set up business in New York City, where, as everyone knew, vice was rampant and evil existed on every street.

As the young man basked in the glory of his victory over the gin mill, his older brother Samuel was fighting the Confederate soldiers. The religious teachings instilled by Polly Comstock had had an effect on Sam, too, who enlisted to fight the curse of slavery. Before the battle of Gettysburg, he was safe behind the lines, working with the commissary department, but the drive to strike down evil compelled him to request duty with a fighting unit. During the first day's carnage Samuel was mortally wounded and died weeks later, humming lines from an old hymn.

Anthony saw it as a sacred duty to pick up the torch dropped by his older brother on the outskirts of the little Pennsylvania village that had become famous overnight. Still not twenty, but with a pair of shoulders that looked like a Percheron's and good health to match his stout physique, Anthony signed up with the Seventeenth Connecticut Regiment of Infantry at Fort Trumbull "to assist in subduing this accursed Rebellion." Later he was transferred with his regiment to Folly Island, S.C. Somewhere along the line he arranged to have the bounty he received for enlisting sent to his family in New Canaan, rejoicing that he could provide "for the little ones at home."

The Union Army was quite different from what Anthony had expected. Men chewed and smoked tobacco, swore shamelessly, and did not appear to mind the fact that there was a shortage of chaplains. A few of his mates called him a Christian as if that were a bad name, but he turned the other cheek. As he soon found out, ignoring a problem never solved it, so he formed a small band of soldiers, all of whom took a solemn pledge not to swear, chew tobacco, or drink liquor.

One day he was detailed to help unload stores, including food and whiskey. Apparently some of his mates found a way to get at the spirits, as soldiers are wont to do, and this event led to a sober entry in Anthony's diary. "Boys got very drunk," he noted. "I did not drink a drop; and yet some were going to whip me. Knocked two over and kept on duty. Touch not. Taste not. Handle not."

For every word dealing with the war itself, there are thousands in this war diary about the waywardness of human nature, the evils of lust, liquor, and laziness, and the writer's sorrow over the lack of church services. This sharing of attention was due in part to Anthony's own interests, but mainly to the Seventeenth Connecticut's being in Florida, where no pitched battles took place and there was only sporadic skirmishing. During one of these petty affairs on a plantation near Jacksonville, Comstock was under fire and duly noted that he heard a bullet "that came very near my head" and caused him to dodge. "But for a kind Providence," he wrote, "would have been killed."

Often suffering from indigestion—he was something of a sybarite when it came to eating—he soldiered through the swamps and palmetto savannahs of nothern Florida, refusing to smoke even to keep away mosquitoes and gnats, building smudges whenever he stopped, and suffering stoically while on the march.

Providence, he recorded, saved his life and lent him

strength to put up with ungodly companions but it served him best when he was given the opportunity to work for the church. Comstock was then in St. Augustine, and an outgoing chaplain left the responsibility for maintaining services in the young soldier's hands. There was no pastor available in the town and few chaplains wanted to add extra duties to their ministry, but Anthony scurried around and often found a preacher who would deliver a sermon in the abandoned church.

This was celestial manna for the young soldier. On such days he would go up into the belfry and ring the bell for five minutes, pray ardently for another five, then ring the bell again for five more minutes. It must have jarred the nerves of soldiers sleeping off Saturday night drunks and they evened the score by staying away from the service.

Anthony's purity of heart and his eagerness to see that the Seventeenth Connecticut was thoroughly exposed to the word of God and took its own sinfulness to heart led to feuding and resentment. One bleak December day he was forced to enter in his diary these strangely written words:

> "Moved up into room alone by myself. After [church] meeting went to go into room, all windows were closed tight, room full of smoke. Bunk ful [sic] of rubbish and loaded with broken Benches, Chairs, etc. Boys were inistiating [sic] me. Had good laugh."

All though the diary so faithfully kept by the boy and later by the man there are frequent notations of how Satan had tempted him, but it is always made clear that by the quick use of prayer or by reading a few verses of the Bible, Beelzebub has been thwarted. These brushes

with sin are never named or described, so the students of
the crusader's early life have to imagine the temptations.
Were they somehow tied to sex? Were women exerting an
attraction he did not wish to confide even to a book kept
under lock and key? No one knows, but sin may have been
written in smaller letters for Comstock than for most men,
as on one occasion he lamented that he had fallen victim
to temptation and had read a novel, spending "part of
the day, foolishly." If wandering so closely to the abyss
disturbed him so much, it must be assumed that he never
felt the pull of more disturbing distractions.

Victory for the Union over the Confederacy was a boon
to young Comstock. It meant not only that he could go
home, unharmed by the war, but that he could get away
from companionship with men for whom the hounds of
hell were panting. Once he could come and go as he wished
he would not have to live with those who took a sarcastic
view of his brand of holiness.

Young Comstock went back to the farm, now mort-
gaged to the hilt. His mother was dead and his father
without drive or impulse to correct conditions. Once again
the young reformer went to clerk in a store, this time in
New Haven, but it was only a stopgap, his heart being set
on a future in New York. While waiting for the opening
he desired, he accepted a government job at Lookout
Mountain in Tennessee, where military buildings were
being converted into a school, but he returned after a few
months, the railroad fare eating up his savings. An older
acquaintance suggested that Anthony seek his fortune in
the big city and gave him $5 for travel expenses. With
the change in his pocket, he stepped off the cars in New
York a few days later, never dreaming that it would one
day tremble at his very voice and blanch at his threat to
clean it up. At that particular moment in his life he

thought only of a career as a dry goods clerk, too humble to imagine himself as the owner of a store.

Whatever drove Anthony Comstock to take up the role of purity's champion exerted itself almost before he had risen from porter in a dry goods shop to the exalted post of salesman. Less than two years after reaching the nation's largest metropolis he had succeeded in dragooning the police into arresting two men who were selling what he was sure were dirty books. More quickly than most men he had found where his deepest interests lay and he had cut the first notches on the weapon he had taken up to do battle with sin.

New York had developed so fast and absorbed so many disparate groups that its underworld had prospered enormously. Between the time when Anna Trow Sommers had stepped ashore from an English ship and that when young Comstock alighted from the train down from New England the city had grown from its site south of 14th Street to a larger area embracing nearly half of Manhattan Island.

Anthony seemed immune to its excitement and vigor. He seemed interested only in making a small income clerking in a store while studying means of preparing himself for the task of ferreting out sin. There was an ample supply of that in Gotham. The young man was stirred by this municipal miasma. Everywhere he turned he seemed to see obscene books and pictures, sinister advertisements, lewd objects and persons.

The youth lost weight working overtime in the dry goods store, and climbed the ladder of responsibility to head clerk within an abnormally short while. But he had time to browse in news stores and bookstalls, proving to himself (as he expressed it to friends) that the publishing world had run amuck producing filth. He had been in town only a short time when he made a citizen's arrest of one bookstore owner. The burning zeal of the crusader was upon him. "Crime stalketh abroad by daylight and public officers wink at it," he wrote in his diary.

This diary, which he had kept so carefully during the war, was now given over to pious notes about the sinful city and how he longed to clean it up. He tried to interest the courts and the police in his campaign but, finding them generally uninterested, he started acting on his own. He threatened a saloon keeper who stayed open on Sundays. This boniface, not liking to be told how to run his business, picketed the boarding house where Comstock stayed, brandishing a revolver. Anthony bought one of his own, kept up the onslaught, and finally drove the bar owner out of business.

It was a small event in a city riddled with high-level crime. City Hall and its supporters were stealing the city blind, building courthouses that cost five and six times what they should have and reaping profits from bribery, kickbacks, and "protection." But the boy from the Connecticut farm was never daunted. Some of his friends thought him crazy on the subject of vice, and his actions in later years tended to support this opinion, but for the time being he was a knight on a white charger, determined to save this second Gomorrah from divine fire.

As things were, the Young Men's Christian Association became disturbed by the laxity of the times. It formed a Committee for the Suppression of Vice and asked Anthony to serve as special agent, though keeping the appointment secret. He would carry the lance while the righteous men of the YMCA stayed safe in the background. The directors thought—probably with good reason—that it might be better if they acted with discreet anonymity.

With an ardor worthy of a greater cause, Comstock

sallied forth, arresting and prosecuting purveyors of smut. He collected his evidence, collared the tradesmen, and then called on the law to take over.

One is tempted to wonder whether his home life helped drive Comstock to spend his time fighting vice. His wife was a mousy creature whose being older than he obsessed her. Her sister Jennie never married and soon moved in with the newlyweds. A child was born to the pair but died soon after. In a fit of depression, Comstock legally adopted a mentally disturbed child whom he saw on a visit to a tenement near Chinatown. Loyal to his wife, he often had to hurry from the house to keep from speaking harshly to her when she expressed concern about what people would say about his crusading. Clearly, he was infinitely tender with her, as this entry in the diary shows:

> Got home and found little Wifey out. Found a dress partly done and I finished it on the machine for her and had the bastings almost out before she came. How she laughed.

This was the man who one day would end Mme. Restell's career—a strange, unwavering fanatic for whom life showed nothing colored gray—only black and white. Before he had been working for the YMCA's vice committee very long he had bulldozed Congress into passing a law banning obscene books and pamphlets. He wrote the law himself. When the dust of the effort had settled, the Postmaster General of the United States swore him in as a special agent of the department, empowered to ride free on all trains, coaches, ships, and carriages carrying the mail and to enforce his own statute.

The *Herald* and other papers across the nation which had profited so richly from the advertisements of quack doctors, useless nostrums, and obscene publications dropped these columns or compressed them rigidly, hoping they would not occasion test cases in the courts. Although Comstock reviled the dailies that ran the ads, he made no move against them. He was too busy with booksellers and news dealers.

As one "sinner" after another was put out of business, fined, or imprisoned, the YMCA's avenging Puritan became one of the celebrities of the city. Hated by thousands, he was praised by perhaps as many, but in the praise hid the germs of eventual trouble. Believing that he could do no wrong, Comstock became ruthless and, possibly, conceited. In this mood he began a collateral crusade against abortionists.

He had less luck in this field than anywhere else. The reason may have been that the laws were weak, but there was also a feeling on the part of a large segment of society that abortion was not the heinous crime that Comstock considered it. All over the country women read of the activities of abortionists, heard whispered stories of neighbors or relatives who had turned to such practitioners in their distress, and said to themselves: "There, but for the grace of God, go I."

Early in May 1873 Comstock went to Albany hoping to prosecute two abortionists, but the authorities in the state capital rebuffed him. The district attorney put the two cases over for several weeks, which annoyed the crusader. Comstock asked why they should not go immediately to a grand jury.

" 'Oh,' he said [the diary notes], 'It won't do to rush these cases through. . . . You are to [sic] energetic, you drive too fast, you would not give us a chance to make a thing. . . .' Away with such men. Give us true men or none at all to fill our offices of Justice."

Ten days later when Anthony was back in New York, the YMCA stepped out of the vice pursuit by the neat trick of incorporating another reform organization, the Society for the Suppression of Vice. Comstock said of the YMCA directors: "They none of them seemed to realize the importance of this Society except to relieve the Committee of its present burden." The situation was complex. Comstock had been so active with the committee that the parent organization found itself spending more time, labor, and money on the one purpose than it wanted or had expected. Some felt that the committee had tainted the image of the YMCA. One director confided to a biographer "that the matters with which he [Comstock] had to deal were too unpleasant to be touched by persons of sensitive feeling, and that more harm was done by stirring up the pool than letting it lie."

Yet by no means did all the directors feel squeamish about the work Comstock undertook. Some of the top philanthropists in the city stood by him, supported him as executive secretary of the new society, and provided the money to keep it alive. Almost as a going-away present for the crusader, the YMCA issued a private report on the old committee's operations. The document was a tribute to Anthony. It showed that he had been responsible for the seizure of 134,000 pounds of obscene books, 14,300 pounds of plates used to print such books, 5,500 decks of indecent playing cards, 3,150 boxes of pills and powders used for contraception, miscarriages, or sexual stimulation, and 60,300 rubber articles which by law should not have been sold or shipped in the mails. Comstock's victims were serving a grand total of twenty-four years and a month in prison, after paying $9,250 in fines.

With this concrete evidence of his success behind him,

Anthony went to court to prosecute a Dr. Selden as an abortionist. The two men met on the courthouse steps and the diary records:

> He came behind me and spit in my face. Then, as I turned, he struck me with his cane, causing the blood to flow freely from my head. I knocked him down and then took him by the collar and handed him over to the Marshall. . . . He is a bad man. . . . This is the first blood I have been called upon to shed for the right. My all, if necessary, if only for my blessed Redeemer.

A few months later Comstock read in the papers that President Grant had pardoned the two abortionists in Albany. It must have broken his spirit a trifle because his activities against abortionists declined for several years. On the other hand this slowdown of the drive against illegal operations may have been a psychological side effect of another situation—one so strangely enticing that Americans watched it unfold with bated breath and constant amazement.

"NEST HIDING"
AND THE
"PAROXYSMAL KISS"

———◄◉►———

Comstock was already up to his muttonchop whiskers in other activities, including libel cases, lawsuits to silence various publications, and arguments with law enforcement officials that stemmed from his crusade. But almost without warning he came to be at grips with two of the most notorious sisters in the country, who printed things in their magazine which Anthony found obscene or revolting. Whether purposefully or not, he also found himself siding with the country's most famous preacher in an adultery case. Some persons voiced insinuations that he sided with Dr. Henry Ward Beecher just to get even with the sisters. He became, to a degree, an actor in what was pure opéra bouffe. It was sensational. It was smut in the pulpit and in the choir loft, and a somewhat Victorian, yet very prurient public was titillated by the whole affair.

It all began when "Commodore" Cornelius Vanderbilt, who did not see fit to explain his actions, set up the sisters Victoria Woodhull and Tennessee Claflin as lady brokers in an office in the financial district. Few sisters in history have been anywhere near as zany as these two.

141

People did not know whether to take the brokers seriously or not. While their male competitors were studying corporate earnings and credit ratings, the sisters were consulting "spirits" or waiting for dreams to guide them. Before they had been in business very long rumors of their past caught up with them. The word *rumors* is used advisedly, because so many people hated these women that it is hard to sift truth from falsehood. These facts, however, seem agreed upon: The sisters were two of a large brood of children born to the Claflins. They grew up in the Middle West, where it was said they operated a hospital, a house of ill repute, and sponsored a movement for women's rights. Victoria married a man named Woodhull at the age of fourteen. When twenty-eight she got a divorce and sometime later married a bewhiskered hero of the Civil War, Colonel James H. Blood of the Sixth Missouri Infantry. By the time the sisters reached New York, they were surrounded by a retinue consisting of parents, both Woodhull and Blood, and various brothers and sisters.

"Right-thinking people" shuddered at the thought that both of Victoria's husbands were living with her. She explained that the first one was an invalid and needed care. As if to confuse everyone further, Victoria and the colonel had been divorced also, simply to uphold their joint belief in free love. Men who had the reputation of being fine judges of feminine beauty said that Tennessee was a truly magnificent woman, but that there was an elfin quality, an electric appeal, that set Victoria apart. She was a speaker who, on almost any subject, could mesmerize an audience, but as she championed such issues as abortion, free love, equality for the sexes, and other novel beliefs, it was little wonder. Theodore Tilton, who was to figure prominently

*Victoria Woodhull, whose advanced views scandalized
the "right-thinking people" of her time.*

in the Beecher case, called Victoria the "Joan of Arc" of the women's movement.

Such a woman would hardly hope to win enough converts just by lecturing, so she founded a weekly magazine called *Woodhull and Claflin's Weekly*, a strange publication filled with articles on the oppression of womankind and tidings of spiritual seances, the whole laced with personal affirmations and supported by financial advertising. Women who considered themselves second-class citizens and any others who had reason to feel hostile to men took Victoria and her words to their minds and bosoms. She was so manifestly brave, personable, and daring!

Early in 1872, under the lead of Susan B. Anthony, Elizabeth Cady Stanton, and other equal-rights advocates, a women's political convention met in New York and nominated Victoria for President of the United States. She accepted the call of the Equal Rights Party— and almost at once stepped on the toes of some of her supporters. While the others stood tongue-tied, she outlined the party's program before the House Judiciary Committee and the women found themselves wondering if they had a tiger by the tail.

Soon there was a serious falling-out. Susan Anthony was all for equal rights, but she did not believe in such sinful causes as free love. The thought of two husbands— one ex- and the other a true marital partner, though a legally divorced one—was too much. At the same time, Victoria's success in winning support for women's suffrage was too valuable to be ignored. Mrs. Stanton argued that the quarrel was really a divisive technique foisted on them by their natural enemies—men. "Let us end this ignoble record and henceforth stand by womanhood," she said. "If Victoria Woodhull must be crucified, let men drive the spikes and plait the crown of thorns."

It was no surprise to anyone to learn that there were men eager and willing to drive the spikes and fashion the crown. One was Anthony Comstock, who agonized every time Victoria's and Tennessee's *Weekly* defended abortion. Another, also a man of action, was Henry C. Bowen, publisher of *The Independent*, a popular religious periodical of the time. Bowen attended the Plymouth Church in Brooklyn, was one of the lay leaders of the congregation, and a stout friend and admirer of Dr. Beecher, whose sermons every Sunday lured hundreds from New York, New Jersey, and Westchester.

Yet another voice was raised against Victoria, but it was a woman's. Harriet Beecher Stowe, sister of the parson, wrote articles for *The Christian Union,* and she too found reason to attack the morals of Victoria and Tennessee.

Mrs. Blood, Miss Woodhull, Victoria née Claflin—all one and the same person—was not the type of woman to take attacks without fighting back. She dashed off an open letter to the *New York Times* promising to expose certain high-level dignitaries who try "to divert public attention from their own iniquity in pointing the finger at me." All the cognoscenti in New York waited expectantly for the explosion to come. They guessed it would involve Dr. Beecher, as stories of his extramarital adventures had been current for several years. To understand the feeling of anticipation, one much know more of the Lord's representative at Plymouth Church.

Everyone agreed that he was the outstanding preacher in the nation. His word was law in hundreds of churchly organizations and in hundreds of thousands of humble homes. He had thundered in support of John Brown, when the latter seized the government armory at Harper's Ferry in a futile attempt to foment a slave rebellion.

Beecher had prayed and threatened, but had remained safely in the north while other lesser figures risked much to help defend Brown at his trial.

In demand at revivals, camp meetings, and pious gatherings all over the country, the chunky, moon-faced preacher, with his great flowing mane of white hair, electrified his audiences not only by his oratory, but by the sheer evidence of physical power. Women in particular thrilled at his every appearance.

On November 2, 1872, Victoria tossed her match into the powder keg. The *Weekly* carried an unusually long article—11½ double-measure, fine-print columns—alleging that Theodore Tilton, the friend of Dr. Beecher and a high-ranking member of the Plymouth congregation, had discovered that his wife had been carrying on an affair with the preacher. The exposé said that Tilton first learned of his wife's infidelity when his little daughter told him of strange carryings-on while he was lecturing out West. Confronting his wife, Tilton won a complete admission of guilt. In a titanic fury the outraged husband ripped the wedding ring from his wife's finger and stomped a photograph of Beecher to shreds before her eyes.

Although she never claimed to be a professional journalist, Victoria Woodhull nonetheless knew how to pull out all the stops. She spoke repeatedly of Beecher's "physical potency" and his "demanding physical nature." As she explained it, Beecher had betrayed the trust of his admirer while being lionized in the Tilton home in Brooklyn Heights during convivial meetings attended by—among others—John Greenleaf Whittier, Wendell Phillips, Horace Greeley of the *Tribune*, and the two suffragists, Mrs. Stanton and Miss Anthony. Beecher, it was asserted, had seduced the impressionable Mrs. Tilton

The eloquent and libidinous Dr. Henry Ward Beecher
of Plymouth Church.

by talking of the virtues of free love. He referred to his dalliance with her as "nest hiding" and argued that it was in no way sinful.

This particular "nest hiding" was not the pastor's first excursion into extramarital affairs, it appeared. Before leading Elizabeth Tilton down the primrose path he had seduced Lucy Bowen, the wife of the very man who edited *The Independent*, in whose pages Victoria Woodhull had been excoriated. Bowen was a man of ambivalent nature. He had no doubt disliked the idea of Beecher's scattering the Bowen home fires, but as a part owner of the Plymouth church property, he did not want to see Beecher's image impaired lest it reduce attendance at the church and harm him financially in other ways.

According to the charge, Lucy Bowen had been seduced by Beecher's mastery of what he called the "paroxysmal kiss," a physical caress of such magnetic quality that she was never quite aware of just when her virtue went up in flames. The titanic anger that had led the young and handsome Mr. Tilton to snatch the wedding ring from his wife's finger subsided in a matter of weeks. The couple tried to patch up the shattered alliance. The wife, a Sunday school teacher, convinced her husband that although she had in truth submitted to Beecher's embraces, she was at heart still "unblemished" and her love for him undiminished.

Tilton tried to forgive not only his wife but also his pastor. It was not easy. Tilton told his tragic story to Bowen, under whom he worked as a writer for *The Independent*. Bowen returned the compliment by telling of his own wife's seduction at the same hands. With this unusual bond, it might have been expected that the two men would have found they had much in common, but they soon disagreed and Bowen fired his assistant.

Dispirited over his unemployment and his inability to care well for his wife and four children, Tilton watched covertly to see if Beecher was keeping his promise to have nothing more to do with Elizabeth. From what he saw, the two lovers were still seeing one another. The carnal flame had not been extinguished. During an argument over his wife's continued infidelity, Tilton told Miss Anthony and Mrs. Stanton the whole story. To these two ladies, the news was a godsend. Whatever the admiration in which they had once held Dr. Beecher, it had drained away by the time he went back on his public word championing suffrage for women.

The reader of today may be excused for thinking of these two famous women—heroines of a great cause—rolling acidulous words on their tongues. How swiftly their high-buttoned shoes must have carried them to Victoria Woodhull's office, there to find that the lady publisher already knew the scandalous facts, but nonetheless enjoying deep pleasure in manifesting their revenge.

Ordinarily *Woodhull and Claflin's Weekly* was not snatched red-hot from the newsboys' hands. It sold for only a few cents a copy; the sisters did not meet their deadlines very regularly. As a matter of record, the previous issue had appeared on the newsstands in July, and the public showed no anxiety for the next. But soon after the November 2 issue came out, scalpers were selling it for $40 a copy to a horde of buyers.

It was the sort of scandal New Yorkers liked: It dealt with a man of international reputation and, what is more, one who was God's agent here below. The fact that the news also involved Victoria and Tennessee was not to be underestimated, for they were known apostles of free love and, in indicting Beecher, they were damning not his adherence to their cult, but his attacks upon them.

149

Tennessee Claflin, co-publisher of Woodhull and Claflin's Weekly.

These criticisms he voiced of the sisters' writings and activities made the public think of such unkindnesses as that shown by the managers of Delmonico's posh restaurant in forbidding women to enter their place without a male escort. How people had chortled when they heard how Tennessee had outfoxed Delmonico's when turned away at the door: She had come back with the cab driver as her companion!

The days went by with charges and countercharges. Publicly, Beecher seemed to ignore the accusations, but secretly he conferred with supporters about ways of bringing pressure to bear on the lady publishers. Meanwhile, further details were feeding the fires that licked at the foundations of Plymouth Church. It appeared that poor little Elizabeth Tilton, frightened by her husband's ire, had had a miscarriage and lost a child whose paternity was not at all certain. Tilton himself stated on many occasions that he was quite sure it was not his child but Beecher's instead.

Victoria Woodhull, to refute insinuations that her facts were inaccurate, pointed to the cuckold husband as the source of the story conveyed by the reliable words of Mrs. Stanton and Miss Anthony. Victoria then really blew the lid off when she wrote that she had interviewed the Plymouth Church dominie himself and had been told by him that marriage was the grave of love.

As the days went by the pages of the *Weekly* were read and passed from hand to hand like a life-and-death message. On perusing it again, hasty readers found Victoria saying that the church in Brooklyn had thrived for a quarter century "augmented and strengthened from the physical amativeness of Henry Ward Beecher." Besides this rather mysterious assertion, certain words compelled them to thumb the dictionary now and again, but it was

151

worth it. There was no doubt as to what Victoria was talking about.

Could anyone do other than smile when Victoria said she printed the charges reluctantly, not from pique but from a feeling of duty—to aid her campaign against the ancient and outworn institution of marriage? Those who saw Victoria as a she-devil espousing a most immoral cause—and there were many—did a little investigating of their own and turned up the fact that at one time Victoria had been something more than a casual friend of Theodore Tilton himself. The sexy young woman who had sought the highest post in the land showed no sign of being embarrassed. She answered this latest accusation by admitting and denying all. In one answer she admitted that "for three months we were hardly out of each other's sight. He slept every night, for three months, in my arms." Later, she perversely contradicted herself, saying their friendship had been completely platonic, and that far from spending alluring hours in her embrace, he "frequently went up the stairs with me to the roof of the house to enjoy the starlight and cool breeze on pleasant summer evenings."

Now how did Anthony Comstock become involved in such sordid matters? The man Heywood Broun and Margaret Leech called in their book "the Roundsman of the Lord" read the attack on Dr. Beecher with a predictable reaction. He saw in the article not an unanswered libel, but a monstrous piece of obscenity. As special agent of the Committee for the Suppression of Vice, he knew just what to do. He called on the United States Attorney to arrest Victoria and Tennessee for sending scurrilous and obscene matter through the mail. It was but one of those little coincidences that peppered the whole scandal that this official happened to be a leading communicant of the

Plymouth Church. He moved with an assurance and swiftness most uncommon and sent marshals to seize the two editors.

The officers found the sisters—dressed in identical costumes—driving up Broad Street in a carriage. Tennessee claimed that when she invited them to ride with them to the United States Commissioner's office, one of them misinterpreted the invitation and plumped himself down in their laps. When the arraignment took place, the sisters found that the charge about obscene matter rested not only on the main article about the Beecher-Tilton case, but also on another in the same issue. In this second piece—one juicy enough to have served as *pièce de résistance* for a later issue had the sisters been more astute —they accused a Wall Street broker, Luther C. Challis, of having disported himself in a most ungentlemanly fashion at a French ball. This, by the way, was not the masked ball at which ladies had been tossed into the air. Challis, the sisters said, had seduced two young "maidens" at the dance, and, blackguard that he was, boasted of it afterward.

When the United States Commissioner set bail at $8,000 each for the sisters they refused to make any effort to raise it. Instead they were driven to the Ludlow Street jail in a show of disdain for the heavy hand of the law. It was 1872—a time in history which most social historians believe to have been fairly enlightened—yet Victoria and Tennessee were locked up for four weeks without hearing or trial after the first routine appearance that brought them to the jail.

This injustice was not unnoticed either by the public or the press. Strangely enough, it was not the New York dailies that took up the torch against this act of oppression. Those champions of innocence hedged or kept silent.

The brave defender was the *Brooklyn Eagle,* which at
that time in its career ran editorials laced equally with
venom and righteousness. The *Eagle* lashed out at the
denial of fair trial, scoffed at the United States in all its
majesty hammering away at two weak women on a purely
local issue, and dusted the dour crusader off with scornful
words about the "irresponsible action of the more zealous
than sensible Comstock."

Anthony must have sensed by now that he was holding
a tiger by the tail. He went over the two articles on which
the arrests were based and decided that the attack on
Challis was the better one on which to base an obscenity
case. By some strange mental process Comstock had come
to the conclusion that the use of the word *virginity* in the
attack on the broker was obscene. He must have wished,
within a few days, that he had bitten his tongue off before
saying so. The attorney for the two women prisoners
quickly accused him of launching an attack on the freedom of the press guaranteed by the Bill of Rights. And
the lawyer had even more fun in showing that the Bible
and Shakespeare, Byron and Voltaire, would come under
the ban voiced by the vice crusader. He read passages
from the Old Testament, including the Song of Solomon
and Deuteronomy, to show how words much more "obscene" occurred repeatedly in those works.

Across the land one could feel a tidal wave of sympathy
for the two imprisoned sisters. Sensible people recoiled at
the thought that the federal government could act against
the two women in order to protect the reputation of one
citizen. And the fact that that one citizen refused to
vindicate himself was not lost on anyone from Maine to
California.

Just when it looked as if the authorities in Washington
would have to move to repair the stupid blunder, Victoria

and Tennessee relieved everybody by accepting bail and quitting the Ludlow Street lockup. Tucked in their reticules was another editorial from the *Eagle* further denigrating the crusader with the one-track mind. Its last words carried a sting:

> As to Mr. Anthony Comstock, we never never heard of him till he 'ranged himself' in legal company with the Claflin sisters as their prosecutor and world-wide advertiser. Even then we never referred to him, for the same reason that we do not refer to last year's flies—he is entirely unimportant.

This editorial, more than any other thing, convinced many New Yorkers that Comstock was a secret agent working in Dr. Beecher's behalf. What admiration they may have had earlier for the reformer was now much weakened. A man who is hated will always find supporters and defenders, but one who is laughed at, lampooned in the daily press, caricatured in the magazines, and sneered at openly in the courtroom loses admirers rapidly.

Six months after Victoria and Tennessee were arrested the indictments against them were dismissed. It was not the end of the Beecher-Tilton cause célèbre by any means, but it gave the people of the city and the country a respite. There had not been as marvelous a show for years, and during the entr'acte, everyone eagerly looked for the next rising of the curtain.

"THE CAN-CAN
À L'EGLISE
DE PLYMOUTH"

Life had gone on as usual in the city while the actors were disporting themselves in the center ring of the circus. A few days before the *Weekly* hit the stands a strange and virulent disease struck many of the city's horses. Within days half the carriages, wagons, and streetcars were absent from their normal haunts because there were no animals to pull them. George Templeton Strong, in his continuing diary, noted the effects of the distemper and said he had seen an ox team on Broadway. "They will have to utilize the elephants and camels of Central Park," he added.

In the excitement over the Beecher story a meeting of the trustees of Columbia College could hardly have been expected to stir much attention, but Strong, one of that body, entered a fact without further comment upon its possible significance:

> Not much done. Reconsidered the reference to a committee of the application of certain young ladies to be admitted as students and unanimously agreed to decline the honor.

The date of this entry was November 3, 1873, a year to the day after Victoria and Tennessee had started their sojourn in jail. Men, it seemed, were not entranced at the idea of equal rights for women.

The depression was now lying heavy on the whole city. Unemployment had mounted grievously; there were breadlines, bankruptcies, suicides, and a Wall Street panic so serious that President Grant came to New York to calm the public fears. Mme. Restell quite clearly survived the panic and depression without ill effects. Her earnings may have dropped a little but she had enough patients to keep her busy. The alleys and side streets behind her house saw muggings and assaults as usual—possibly more than usual—but these events went unnoticed in the big mansion on the corner of the Avenue.

More likely to have attracted her attention was the news that Big Bill Tweed, whom the Tammany Tiger had assumed was too powerful to attack, was found guilty of fraud and sentenced to twelve years in jail. This was something like the handwriting on the wall. Was reform becoming a power in the city? When Ned Stokes shot Jim Fisk dead on the main staircase of the Grand Central Hotel, partly because of financial battles but even more because the voluptuous Josie Mansfield had quitted Fisk's arms for Stokes's, that was something closer to Mme. Restell's normal concerns. Not that she approved of violence. Small annoyances were in the forefront of the abortionist's mind; the city was paving Fifth Avenue with cobblestones and had about reached her place, but the rest of the Avenue up to Central Park was still a dirt road. In the winter it was full of ruts and potholes and in the summer she had to keep the windows closed on the west and north sides of the house because of the dust blowing around.

Mary Mason Jones had finished building the group of houses she called Marble Row near 58th Street and many people were remarking on their beauty, due largely to the change of material from the usual brownstone or sandstone. When Mme. Restell learned that the fine location above her corner had cost Mrs. Jones's father only $1,500 in 1825, she was put out. Her own site had cost a great deal more because everybody seemed bent on moving up the Avenue, and some were saying that before the northward push ended houses would be built along the road facing the park way up in the Sixties and Seventies.

As a widow, the female "physician" seldom left her mansion except for a drive when weather permitted. The papers were full of stories about social events her neighbors took part in, but she sat alone with her thoughts. The Grand Duke Alexis of Russia had arrived on a state visit, riding triumphantly up Broadway and forcing the omnibuses to change their routes. Rustics and lion-hunters gathered by the thousands to see a real live Russian grand duke, and he came to spend his evenings at houses whose bright lights she could see.

About the same time *Aïda* was given its premiere in America and the papers said there was not an inch left for a hungry mouse in the Academy of Music. P. T. Barnum, the ever-youthful, ever-dynamic showman, opened with success his Great Roman Hippodrome on 27th Street between Madison and Fourth Avenues, but there was also a real-life exhibit to rival his latest attractions when King Kalakaua of the Sandwich Islands arrived in the city and put up at the Windsor Hotel. The king took a ride in the park in a sleigh whenever there was enough snow, unable to get over his amazement at the white stuff.

All in all, despite the panic and the lean months that followed, New York—or at least its well-to-do—enjoyed a gay time. A group of prominent bachelors held an elaborate masquerade at Delmonico's and the next day the occasion had been given the unpleasant title of "the Bouncers' Ball." The name signified that many of the men and women present were "not heretofore considered among the socially elect."

The Astor and Vanderbilt ladies who decided who "were" and who "were not" and who besides were really beyond the pale were shocked that Delmonico's would countenance such doings. These ladies thought another party, called the Swan Banquet, that had preceded the rowdy one much more in keeping with the tastes of society. At the Swan dinner the guests sat around an artificial lake built within an oval table while four majestic swans, borrowed for the evening from Prospect Park in Brooklyn, swam lazily about, nibbling on pieces of rolls tossed to them by the crowd.

If Mme. Restell was indifferent to these doings, neither did they affect the man who was to be her undoing. Anthony Comstock was still busy raiding bookstores, while also giving attention to the development of the Beecher-Tilton imbroglio. That case showed no signs of dying down and the vice crusader, although licking his burned fingers, could not keep away from the fire.

All the while the Claflin sisters were far from remorseful, nor were they hiding their lights under a bushel. Victoria in particular traveled up and down the land from one lecture hall to another, attacking both Beecher and Bowen. Then, as ever, full of courage, they reprinted the entire spicy edition of the *Weekly*, pleasing everybody except a few dealers who still hoped to get high prices for their first editions.

It must be said for the congregation at Plymouth Church that most members remained loyal to Dr. Beecher.

They kicked Tilton out, calling him a string of bad names —for a church group, at least—and he returned the compliment by issuing a new statement detailing every incident in the now famous argument. After months of staying aloof from the hassle, Dr. Beecher finally moved off dead center—not by a daring step: He appointed a committee. Six well-known members of the congregation were asked to investigate what he termed "rumors, insinuations and charges." The deck, one could say, was cleared—but also stacked.

The only point of interest during the committee's inquiry came when Elizabeth Tilton, bent on defending Beecher, walked out of her home and left her husband and children. When Tilton swore an affidavit of his wife's seduction, Beecher denied it and called it blackmail but he did not bring suit. As the papers across the country printed every scrap of news they could ferret out, the affair dragged on. The six-man committee finally exonerated Dr. Beecher of all wrongdoing. The whitewashing was not unexpected.

Tilton, now jobless, deserted by his wife, and thrown out of the church, still had courage enough to sue the preacher for alienation of his wife's affections. Coincidentally with the filing of the papers, he announced to the press that even if he won he would not accept a penny in financial damages, although the Good Lord knew he could use a little money.

This action electrified the nation. People sensed that here was a brave man, fighting the establishment and willing to risk the little he had left—his reputation. These same people had been talking and thinking about the earlier obscenity suit brought by Comstock against the *Weekly,* and had come to the conclusion that it was a sorry day for individual freedom when the power of the

United States government could be thrown against two sisters in a case dealing with purely local matters. Not everyone ran a fever. George Templeton Strong, a bit blasé, perhaps, or just wanting to say "a plague on both your houses," made an entry in his diary while the case moved toward trial:

"The can-can *à l'eglise de Plymouth* is not yet danced out but grows faster and more furious."

A little further along he jotted down a hilarious anecdote totally unconnected with the Beecher-Tilton case, but indicating strongly that in England, at least, the clergy did not possess the aura of complete respectability taken for granted in this country:

> The Rev. Morgan Dix just returned on the Cunarder *Russia*. While in London he went to the illustrious Poole's to order some clothes. The urbane salesman said, "Certainly, sir, with great pleasure, sir, but then we don't take orders, sir, from strangers, sir, without some kind of reference, sir." "Oh, ah—of course, very proper," said the Rev. Morgan Dix, and produced from his pocket a letter of introduction from Bishop Potter to the Archbishop of Canterbury. The salesman hummed and hesitated and then said, "Yes, sir, a most flattering endorsement, sir. It would carry great weight in clerical circles, sir, but it won't do here, sir." So the Rev. Morgan Dix had to go into the City and get a letter from his banker.

Early in January 1875 the trial opened in Brooklyn City Court. Outside, queues formed daily. Bankers and clerks, merchants and salesmen, actors and housewives hoped to squeeze inside. Reporters from papers across the land jammed the press section, their wired reports keeping millions palpitating—or so the writers believed. Some papers issued special editions devoted entirely to the case. The printing shops of the city worked all night producing a rash of pamphlets authored by the Lord only knows who, but bought in a twinkling.

Twelve men were chosen as jurors, eager, possibly, but not able to guess that they would listen to one of the longest trials in American history. Tilton told his story, which was supported by other witnesses. His wife denied she had been seduced, and tried without much success to explain why she was changing her earlier story of bliss in Beecher's arms. Day after day opposing counsel sought to break down the testimony unfavorable to their clients until it seemed as if the truth would never come out.

No wonder Mrs. Stanton wrote of the "impossibility of securing justice for anyone when money can be used against him." On the day Beecher himself took the stand the ladies of his congregation sent huge bouquets of flowers to him in the courtroom, but the sweet scent of the blossoms did not hide the odor of dissembling, side-stepping, and contrived forgetfulness.

The eloquent pastor who could make his audiences laugh or cry at will, who thundered righteously against the iniquities of slavery and the evil of the Confederate cause, and who still packed Plymouth Church every Sunday was a sad witness in his own behalf. Even to his friends he seemed hesitant and to others a miserable transgressor.

On this stage Anthony Comstock had but a minor role. It was probably fortunate for the crusader that he remained mostly in the background, for many secondary figures were tarred with the brush used by editorial writers against Dr. Beecher. It would have done Comstock little good to be discussed, for example, in the editorial with which Colonel Henry ("Marse Henry") Watterson of the *Louisville Courier-Journal* laid Dr. Beecher low: The Brooklyn preacher, wrote Watterson, is "a dunghill covered with flowers."

The trial that had opened in January's bitter cold ended in July's oppressive heat. There was no verdict. The twelve jurymen failed to arrive at a decision and were excused by the judge. Depending upon whose side you were, the mistrial was a victory for Tilton or an acquittal for Dr. Beecher. The preacher took it for the latter, and went on preaching and lecturing at never less than $1,000 an appearance. It was said that many men went to hear the clergyman just to see what sort of fellow he was in the flesh. It was also said that more than one lady gladly paid to gaze upon his commanding figure, dreaming the while of things ungodly.

As for Comstock, he was still busy with Congress, getting through a stronger obscenity law while the Beecher affair dragged to its unsatisfactory finale. All the things the press had said about him for hounding Victoria Woodhull and Tennessee Claflin left him unmoved. He may have winced at just one accusation: that he was afraid to tackle a really powerful periodical. This charge of cowardice would be thrown at him years later while he prosecuted petty abortionists and paid no attention to Mme. Restell. But he had learned that there are times when it is best to keep a tightly buttoned lip, and he never answered the allegations of the press.

It can hardly be doubted that the majority of the trustees of the YMCA were happy they had eased out the vice crusade from their jurisdiction and lodged it with an entirely independent group. As it was, the "Y" came in for a healthy share of criticism. Many newspapers accused it of being "a Jesuit crowd" working to reinstate the terrors of the Spanish Inquisition. But dear, sweet, irrational, mercurial, but always articulate Victoria Woodhull drew the most blood when she referred to it, as she did for many years, as "the Young Men's Christian (Christ forgive the connection) Association."

Much earlier, during the trial of the two sisters, Comstock had written a comment in his diary that was pertinent when the Beecher-Tilton foofaraw was ended. It reveals how immune he was to criticism, how sure he was of the ultimate righteousness of his crusade:

> I am called "obscene man." Well, what matters. Words hurt no one and as the course he is pursuing in maligning me at every point [referring to the defense counsel] is injuring his clients and not myself or my cause, I have no reason to complain. . . . Sometimes we serve the Master as well by "bearing patiently" as any other way.

A thick skin was what made Anthony Comstock such a formidable foe. Convinced in his heart that he was invariably doing the Lord's work, he went through life without self-doubt or the questioning of one's aims, which most normal men at times engage in.

Comstock, being busy, took no notice of the way in which his friends and foes of the Woodhull-Claflin and Beecher-Tilton escapades pursued their careers. Beecher's success on the lecture circuit did not seem to him important enough to warrant comment in his diary. He would have chopped off his right hand before noting down that Victoria and Tennessee had moved to England, there to marry brilliantly: Tennessee married a baronet and Victoria a wealthy banker.

Three years after the Beecher trial ended, Elizabeth

Tilton changed her story yet again in a letter published in virtually every paper in America.

"The charge, brought by my husband," she wrote, "of adultery between myself and the Reverend Henry Ward Beecher was true. The lie I had lived so well the last four years had become intolerable to me."

Again, Comstock paid no attention. His post, as he put it, was "at the sewer mouth of society." If ever a man had a one-track mind, it was Anthony. Even those in his curious profession, who were trying to stamp out lust, suppress suggestive books and pictures, and prosecute publishers of dime novels, found that he went rather too far.

The superintendent of the Woman's Christian Temperance Union's Department of Purity in Literature and Art in New York State summed it up neatly:

> The trouble with Mr. Comstock is that he thinks no one has a right to work for social purity without first obtaining permission from him.

It could have been that Comstock was reacting—as other prominent men have been known to do—to the headlines he was gaining. He was no longer that saintly soldier trying to bully chaplains into preaching still another sermon in another chapel. He was no longer the unknown dry goods salesman getting storekeepers and saloon owners arrested for being open on the Sabbath. Nor was he quite as naive as when he was first accidently sucked into defending Dr. Beecher while bringing down the wrath of God and the courts on Victoria and Tennessee.

Now he was a man whose name was known across the land—both hated and ridiculed as well as admired. Indeed a little of the Beecher charisma had rubbed off on Anthony's garments. He was in the limelight, famous or infamous, depending on the point of view. In a very few years he would move against the woman called the most evil in New York City, but right now neither the reformer nor the abortionist knew their careers were like a railroad track, the lines disappearing in the distance but growing closer all the time.

EVERYONE WENT
DRIVING
IN CENTRAL PARK

Although military men and government officials drew crude maps of New Amsterdam almost as soon as the fort was built and a few houses were erected outside the walls, the first accurate drawing of the Dutch outpost on Manhattan followed these by several decades. Known as the Castello Plan, from the summer villa outside Florence where it was discovered, it was a copy of a Dutch map showing not only streets and parade grounds and docks, but the precise location of every dwelling, together with its owner.

By one of those coincidences that enliven history, the house that was closest to the main gate of the fort belonged to a Dutch woman named Trijin Jonas. She had no official position with the Dutch West India Company, which governed the colony, and there is almost no mention of her in early documents, but she was one of the most important members of the little community at the lower tip of Manhattan Island. She was the colony's midwife—the first of her profession in what was to become New York State.

So far as is known, no whisper of scandal ever touched Mevrouw Jonas. She went about the settlement with her basket of bandages scorched with a hot iron, although germs where not a known factor at the time, goose-grease ointment and laudanum pills, bringing babies into the world and nursing their mothers back to health. Legends have been built around figures like Peter Minuit, who purchased Manhattan Island from the Indians, peg-legged Peter Stuyvesant, and fat Wouter Van Twiller but not about humble old Trijin Jonas. Yet to the ordinary soldier, farmer, and worker, and their wives, Trijin was something of a saint. Two hundred years later, where the Indians had roamed north of the Dutch stockade at Wall Street, another midwife served her patients well also—those of them who wanted their babies. Mme. Restell cared for hundreds of women who took their babies away from the house on Fifth Avenue after their accouchement and never spoke any evil of the midwife. On such occasions Mme. Restell doubtless felt as justified as Trijin Jonas had.

On ordinary days, when four o'clock in the afternoon struck, the woman "physician" stepped briskly into her carriage and headed for the east concourse of Central Park—a throughfare that led from the spot where the Hotel Plaza now stands to the Mall, a mile or more into the park. Curious people with nothing better to do crowded along the grassy borders of the carriage drive, trying to recognize the fashionable folk as they wheeled past. The carriage was the most popular vehicle but there were many other varieties. The barouche was larger than the victoria and both enabled the occupants to be easily seen. The brougham was more boxlike, with sides and glass-topped doors, which afforded privacy for those

The fashionable folk turn out for a drive in Central Park.

within. The phaeton was lighter and faster and carried a groom perched on a high seat behind the body of the vehicle.

Not unnaturally the most proper ladies tended to ride in fancy equipages, while those with less standing in the community clung to conventional, even old-fashioned types. There were exceptions, if only to prove the rule, and the most marked example was the preference of truly distinguished residents whose forebears had fought with Washington in the War of Independence, who clung to the shadows within their broughams.

So, on any sunny afternoon, the eager watchers would see young ladies of impeccable background whizzing by in dogcarts (which had nothing to do with dogs) or in phaetons, their laughter clearly audible and their pretty parasols twirling like pinwheels.

In contrast, stars of the theater and others whose names were tinged with scarlet went driving in highly decorous carriages—usually a victoria. Mme. Restell's carriage was all black, as sedate as a nun's habit. Josie Woods, whose brothel on Clinton Place near University Place was reputedly the most exclusive in town, rode out in a similarly dignified vehicle.

No one among the bystanders, unless they knew these latter ladies, would have guessed that they were anything but rich New York women with lily-white characters. At night the demimondaines moved in a shadowy world of which the other segment of society spoke only with meaningful looks, but in the bright sunlight of a summer afternoon in Central Park, no clear distinction was possible.

Mme. Restell never overdressed. A couturier would have seen at once that what she wore was of the best—never in bad taste, never showy. Josie Woods, who was a few years younger, was a woman of striking beauty, her raven-hued, shiny hair framing a face with finely chiseled features. Looking like the wife of a Spanish grandee, she was always turned out elegantly in rich silks set off by sparkling diamonds.

Mme. Restell's proper deportment in public brought her no social acceptance. This was particularly odd in the middle of a century when New York morals were paper-thin. Jay Gould and Jim Fisk had milked millions from gullible investors by manipulating the finances of the Erie Railroad. "Boss" Tweed had robbed the city of other millions by building overpriced courthouses and pocketing the kickbacks. Hardly a railroad was operating that had not taken the public for a ride other than on its rails. The law finally caught up with Tweed, but the others and their friends were welcomed in the best houses, asked to serve on cultural and philanthropic boards, and never ostracized. Only Mme. Restell remained beyond the pale.

Outwardly, New York was changing, although daily life went on as usual. As the residential district moved north, so did the nightlife areas. Lower Sixth Avenue inherited many of the bawdy houses and gambling places. The West Twenties and Thirties had districts known as Satan's Circus and the Tenderloin which lured those formerly attracted to Water Street and Greene Street.

The christening of the Tenderloin came about in an odd way. A police precinct captain named Alexander S. Williams, better known as "Clubber" Williams, had spent all his career in quiet residential districts far from mid-Manhattan. Then he was given the twenty-ninth precinct, scene of the criminal activities. Some weeks after, when he had had time to familiarize himself with the area of his responsibility, he was seen strolling along Broadway, smiling like a Cheshire cat. A friend asked why this was. "Well," answered "Clubber," "I've been transferred. I've had nothing but chuck steak for a long time, and now I'm going to get a little of the tenderloin."

From that day the district was always known as the Tenderloin. How much the graft amounted to is guesswork, but the history of one of the worst dives affords some measure of comparison. Known as the Haymarket, it was a combination dance hall, brothel, and an American version of the Parisian peep shows. It was deprived of its license regularly but always managed to reopen for business; the trick was turned by paying off someone in authority.

Women were admitted without charge at the Haymarket, but men paid a quarter to get past the bouncers at the front door. Inside the guests danced, and when they tired of that, they watched a girlie show that put on a raunchy variation of the French can-can. Those who grew bored with these entertainments chose partners and retired upstairs. In the small hours of the morning when unsophisticated sightseers had gone back to their hotel rooms and when the theater was almost obscured by cigar smoke, the girls returned to the stage to dance the can-can again. Rumor had it that during the late night show they dispensed with undergarments.

"Diamond Jim" Brady was a frequent visitor at the Haymarket, but associates noticed two things about the big-time spender when he left the more elegant parts of town for an evening in the Tenderloin: He never took Lillian Russell with him and he never wore his twenty-carat diamond stickpin, cufflinks, or rings. Even "Diamond Jim" suspected that for all his close friendship with police bigwigs he might never come out of the Haymarket with his jewels.

The proprietors of this notorious dive finally worked out a system for avoiding police interference and the subsequent lifting of their license. They announced that the theater and dance hall would be available almost exclusively to organizations wishing to sponsor their own entertainment. It was a lie, a crass subterfuge, but it worked for a good while.

The biggest headache for the management was to figure out new names for the shadow organizations hiring the hall. Each night a new group would supposedly hire the Haymarket, and before the farce was over such groups as the Brooklyn Cycle and Nature Lovers Club, the Yorktown Yodeling and Mountain Society, and the West Side Violin and Euchre Society had each sponsored an evening.

With New York a wide-open city, with sin and graft and political conspiracy the accepted way of life in Gotham, it is easy to understand Mme. Restell's irritation at the criticism aimed at her. She could hardly be unaware of the censure. Even in her rather isolated circumstances she heard rumors of impending trouble. Stories of her nefarious behavior were rife. One of them had to do with an event supposed to have happened way back when she was living at 160 Chambers Street. The tale—never substantiated—was that a young woman under the abortionist's care had died by reason of criminal negligence. No one was ever quoted, but "they" said a warrant had been issued for Mme. Restell's arrest but never executed: She had bribed a judge with $100,000 in cash.

Even though Mme. Restell was a wealthy woman a bribe of this size seems unlikely. But rumor scorns facts and does not need them to be believed. People took it for granted that the lady "physician" was beyond the reach of prosecution.

One of her neighbors held a different view. He was Isaiah Keyser, a sort of anachronism who ran a small truck garden diagonally across Fifth Avenue from the Restell place. His little plot extended from 51st to 52nd Street, on a block later made famous when William K. Vanderbilt built two ornate stone mansions there four years after Mme. Restell died. One was for himself, the other for his married daughter. Still later than that the site was occupied in part by the famous DePinna store, where later generations of wealthy New Yorkers bought their clothes.

Keyser had a three-story frame house on his property, but the rest of his land was given over to raising vegetables. His produce was so high-class he never had to look for customers; he sold most of his stuff to families living on the Avenue.

The Fifth Avenue farmer delivered his produce regularly at Mme. Restell's side door and found her a good customer and a quick payer. If he knew what went on in the upper bedrooms, it never bothered him. When some of the other homeowners in the area tried to buy her out, the farmer took no part in the plan. He may even have figured that whoever moved in might not be so reliable a customer.

During the decade in which Anna Trow Restell was finally brought to court by Anthony Comstock, a small group of writers and reformers were running high fevers over New York's international reputation as a shameless metropolis. Many an author saw a chance to cash in on writings about the seamy side of New York life. Most of these works were cleverly designed to get the most out of the subject. Raising eyes and hands to heaven, the writers could fill their pages with details otherwise unacceptable. The readers, having scanned every line and drooled at every line drawing, could then be expected to say, "What a sinful place!"

The *National Police Gazette* delighted in printing articles about innocent girls who came in from the farm and were soon seduced into a licentious life, or of rich men's sons who, corrupted by the pretty inmates of the better bagnios, lost all grip on themselves and wound up in the waterfront dives.

There seemed to be no shortage of authors, or paper, or readers. Matthew Hale Smith wrote a book called *Sunshine and Shadow in New York* and George Ellington turned out another two years later entitled *The Women of New York* to join the earlier mentioned volume by

Rev. James McCabe, *Lights and Shadows of New York Life.*

These volumes, and many others, followed one plan: They included chapters on such praiseworthy institutions as the churches and missions; they described the new buildings and discussed such topics as public transportation, the railroads, and Wall Street. But somewhere in the books were fat chapters about the city's night life, its organized crime and vice, and the perils confronting innocent visitors from the hinterland. The authors excused themselves in advance by pointing out that they were only "unveiling the facts truthfully and boldly," ostensibly as a public service. Artists collaborated with the writers, turning out pen and ink sketches of well-fed young women luring country bumpkins into their arms by posing as artists' models or as dancing partners in the concert-hall saloons.

Ellington went even farther. In his preface, after making it clear that his exposures were done in the public interest, he expressed the hope that the women of the city "may yet become as celebrated for their virtues as those of rural districts throughout the land." Poor Ellington! He must never have attended a rural pie supper or taken a sleigh ride in the remoter country districts.

One feature of these books is worth noting: The illustrations—and they were most plentiful—showed women in many daring poses, but seldom were their lower limbs much exposed. It would have been altogether too crude, at a time when dresses swept the floor and ladies were not imagined as possessing lower extremities. To make up for the omission the women in these well-thumbed exposés were all blessed with magnificent busts, whose pneumatic opulence need not be hidden by high-necked dresses.

These things being so, it is no wonder that George

Templeton Strong was moved to coin a phrase when discussing a new musical that opened at Niblo's Garden. He confessed in his diary that he had been among the men-about-town who went to catch an early performance of *The White Fawn*. Many of the actresses were costumed as soldiers or pages and their skirts (they wore skirts in *this* army) ended far above the knee. Strong dismissed the musical as "the most showy, and least draped, specimen of what may be called the *Feminine-Femoral* School of Dramatic Art."

When Walt Whitman, whose life was seldom held up as an example to the youth of his era, wrote that life in the city was "pervaded with flippancy and vulgarity, low cunning, infidelity, and everywhere an abnormal libidinousness," you had to assume that what the other authors had been describing was sheer understatement.

"A BLOODY ENDING
TO A BLOODY LIFE"

In 1875 a group of artists and their philanthropic backers founded the Art Students' League, an educational institution for the training of young American painters and sculptors. Like any other reputable art school, there were life classes where students learned to draw what many believe to be the most beautiful handiwork of God—the nude female form.

To Anthony Comstock this was an affront. He reacted to the school's establishment as if he had been jolted by a powerful electric current. It never occurred to him that the naked figure had been an important part of the greatest art since man first learned to sketch on cave walls with a burnt stick.

On several occasions he barged into the League's rooms on 23rd Street to check on the classes. Using his powers as a postal inspector, he confiscated a bulletin published by the school because it reproduced sketches of nudes done by students. In his raids on stores selling art supplies, books, and paintings he seized hundreds of pictures he deemed obscene. Some of them were exactly that, and

177

found no champions in the ranks of art lovers, but so tormented was the reformer's soul about the dangers lurking in the undraped female figure that he even seized reproductions of paintings the whole world had acknowledged as masterpieces.

Years later, long after the death of Mme. Restell, he raided the League again and excoriated officials for permitting copies of that innocent—and not very great—work *September Morn* to circulate. From the beginning of the League's existence Anthony was a hornet, irritating and threatening everyone.

Pressed for an explanation of his puritanical feelings about nudes, Comstock gave an answer that is good material for today's psychologists. He said:

> No one reveres the female form more than I do. In my opinion there is nothing else in the world so beautiful as the form of a beautiful maiden woman —nothing. But the place for a woman's body to be—denuded—is in the privacy of her own apartments with the blinds drawn.

Anthony's jousting with windmills did not escape the newspapers' notice. Editorial writers poked fun at him, quoting his opinions, and a large segment of the population thought the reformer was going too far.

Did this criticism hasten the reformer's decision to move against the lady in the fine house at Fifth Avenue and 52nd Street? There is no proof it did or did not. It is extremely likely, however, that the loss of face he suffered in the Beecher-Tilton case motivated him. Perhaps even more potent was the ridicule heaped upon him for behaving like a bull in the city's moral china shop. His diary gives no inkling of the factors prodding him to action. His record in attacking other abortionists in Albany,

Chicago, and Boston was very poor, but he evidently decided it was essential for him to try to catch Mme. Restell. It could have been that he thought a dramatic arrest might brighten his slightly tarnished escutcheon. Certainly there was information at hand to support his belief that Mme. Restell was the queen of her kind in the country. If the *Herald Presbyter*, a religious publication in Cincinnati, Ohio, could state in its columns a few days after the Restell arrest that she was worth $1,500,000, Anthony Comstock—on the scene in New York City—would have been aware that he was after big game.

The special agent for the Society for the Suppression of Vice told some of his associates that he had decided "to go after" the female "physician" only because many lesser figures he put in jail had accused him of not daring to arrest her. In the final analysis, the reasons behind his actions do not matter. He had ignored this "most evil woman in New York" for better than a decade. Now he made up his mind to act.

Like a general plotting a battle, Anthony laid his plans for the assault with methodical attention to detail. He began his attack by writing several letters to the abortionist, asking her counsel and assistance in a personal matter of great gravity. These letters no longer exist, naturally, but they must have shown the master hand, trained by years of just such undertakings. To make them more believable—some newspaper writers said later —he had the letters mailed from a small town in his home state of Connecticut; but here again hard evidence is lacking.

Then on a cold wintry day in February 1878 came a knock at Mme. Restell's door. Her maid invited the visitor in. He was a healthy-looking man in a dark suit and overcoat, shoes that resembled a policeman's, clean linen, and a black bow tie. He was thirty-four at the time, and wore full muttonchop whiskers, as well as a mustache that half-hid thin, straight lips. Why Mme. Restell did not recognize his well-publicized features is nothing short of a real mystery.

When he saw Mme. Restell he told her a harrowing story of family poverty. As she listened to the sort of tale she had heard many times—particularly in her early days on Greenwich Street—he explained that he had several children and that his wife was now pregnant with another. He humbly sought advice and counsel.

The abortionist, as was her way, suggested that he return at a later time. Perhaps she sensed something wrong. Perhaps she was simply being routinely careful. At any rate, Comstock did return a few days later and, if anything, his tale of misery was even more heartrending. Mme. Restell listened sympathetically and then offered him medicine which she assured him would bring about "the desired results." That was all the crusader needed. He made himself known and showed the abortionist his special identification as agent for the vice society and his credentials as a special operative for the Post Office. He had everything ready—a warrant in his pocket and policemen stationed outside. These he called in and together they searched the entire mansion. They found pills, powders, bottles, and certain instruments commonly used by obstetricians.

If Comstock had staged his raid before 1873 Mme. Restell might have gone free. The law at that time held that the state must prove the instruments had actually been used by the suspected abortionist. Later the law was tightened and the mere presence of such instruments in the house or office of anyone but an obstetrician was prima facie evidence of wrongdoing. Mere possession was all

Comstock needed to hold the lady "physician" as a criminal.

A few days later a second warrant was issued for Mme. Restell's arrest, and on February 11 Comstock served it on her. She summoned her carriage, invited the reformer to ride downtown with her, and sped off for the Tombs with all the dignity of England's Queen going to a lawn party. No one on the sidewalks seemed aware of the odd couple sitting together in the carriage.

Somewhat later, when the story was the talk of the town, the rumor ran about that Mme. Restell had offered Comstock $40,000 if he would just step down from the carriage and forget all about her. But, then again, the pair may only have exchanged small talk about the weather.

Her footman handed the lady down, leaving the portly crusader to scramble to the street by himself. The pills and instruments were locked up as evidence in the district attorney's office and a preliminary hearing staged within a few minutes. Comstock testified that he had found the wife of one of New York's prominent citizens in one of Mme. Restell's upstairs rooms, but he did not divulge her identity. Nevertheless, the next few days must have been terrible ones for the woman in question.

When he was shown the instruments found by Comstock, Judge Kilbreth held Mme. Restell in $10,000 bail. Without batting an eye, the prisoner reached into her reticule and drew out $10,000 in United States gold bonds. Judge Kilbreth refused the offer, insisting on a regular bail bond. This took a little time and the abortionist had to spend several days in the Tombs Prison.

In her hour of need, several of her friends stood by her. Dressed to the nines, they drove to the prison in their fancy carriages, accompanied by uniformed attendants, and there offered their assistance. Some of the people who saw them drive up to the grim place may have had fleeting thoughts that the abortionist would once again bribe or threaten her way out of her toils. But this time her enemy was Anthony Comstock and it meant a different predicament.

After bail had been arranged, Mme. Restell rode home, the black ostrich plumes on her hat waving defiantly in the winter wind. This time the crowds on the sidewalks near the prison knew who the passenger in the victoria was and, not liking the sneaky way Anthony Comstock had tricked her, cheered her lustily. Now they saw her as the victim, not of a legitimate prosecution, but of a cheap persecution.

The abortionist was not inclined to give in. She retained excellent legal counsel for her defense and during most of March there was a barrage of legal maneuvers: show cause orders, applications for writs of certiorari, and a trial was set for April 1, obviously by a calendar clerk without a sense of humor.

In the mansion where the New York office of Japan Air Lines and the Plymouth Shop now occupy the site of the abortionist's third and finest home, there was no longer the old defiance. None of the things that had helped before were useful against the bulldog determination of Anthony Comstock.

The proffered bribe—if in fact it was tendered—had fallen on deaf ears. The intercession of her well-to-do friends had done nothing, and the old standby—the threat to divulge horrible secrets involving socially influential families—bore no fruit.

Consequently, these were days of terror not only for the abortionist. It was said in certain government circles that Comstock had found a little black book, presumably containing the names of women who had had illegal operations performed at 52nd Street. This story was embroidered until it was believed that James Gordon Bennett, the fiery publisher, was trying to get the list so as to print the names in the *Herald*. "Hundreds of fashionable folk quaked when they learned Comstock had taken hold of her," reported one newspaper. "They dreaded that when she found herself driven to the wall, bereft by friends afraid to help her, there would be State's evidence given about their affairs, and all the skeletons in the closets would be brought out to public view."

The sword of Damocles never fell. On the morning of April Fool's Day Judge Kilbreth donned his black robes and went to the bench. The courtroom was jammed with expectant humanity, New Yorkers waiting to hear justice meted out to the doyenne of wicked women. Minutes dragged by and nothing happened. Then a messenger handed the judge a note which he read with evident amazement. He put it down and announced that the defendant had committed sucide. There would be no trial.

Because of the date many thought it was all a monstrous joke, but this surmise was soon dispelled. One lawyer turned to an associate and said: "Nolle pross'd by Death." Within a few hours most of the truth was known.

Sometime after midnight, according to the coroner, Mme. Restell had made her decision. Alone in the big house except for her seven servants, the woman Anthony Comstock had tricked rose from her bed and tiptoed down the hall to the bathroom. She carried a carving knife taken from the butler's pantry earlier in the night. Turning on the water in the bathtub, she slipped off her peignoir and then her nightgown. She stood unclad while the water ran into the tub—a stout figure, alabaster white except for face and hands, surprisingly firm for a woman of sixty-seven. She stepped into the filled tub, sat down, and drew the knife blade across her throat in one swift stroke.

That self-ordained pamphleteer Bishop Huntington, who hastened to get his story into print, described the scene in far more lurid prose. Perhaps the fact that he knew nothing at all about the details made it easier for him to be eloquent. At any rate, these are the bishop's words, but by no means all of them:

> Come with us, reader, two hours past midnight. Let us enter this costly and magnificent mansion of brownstone, raising itself in the most aristocratic portion of New York City. Now you stand in a palace . . . pure white Carrara marble . . . what richness, what regal splendor! . . . Hush, be very still. What was that? A noise upstairs. . . . She steps out of her bedroom. In her hand she clutches . . . what? That's the gleam of a large knife, with an edge like a razor. She glides with noiseless steps along the hall to the bathroom. There is no haste as she disrobes. . . . How steady her fingers as they undo the exquisite gold button at her throat and how calmly the garment is dropped to the floor, and she stands just as she entered the world, so is she going to leave it. She steps over the side of the tub into the water, sits down . . . reaches out her hand . . . and draws forth the knife. She knew where to cut, and the carving knife drops from her dying hands with a little plash into the water, slides from her breast . . . to the bottom of the tub. And now the water is blushing scarlet at the dreadful deed. . . . With her own hand she has quashed Comstock's indictment. . . . She had appealed to the Supreme Court of Heaven.

The upstairs maid found the body of her mistress some hours later when the water had turned not only scarlet but cold. She called the police and they summoned the coroner. That official made out the necessary papers and in them noted that the button which had fastened Mme. Restell's nightgown was an exquisite diamond—not gold, as the bishop imagined.

Anthony Comstock showed no regret when told of the suicide. Sure that his own actions were right in the eyes of God, he said coldly: "A bloody ending to a bloody life." For the first time in years, all over town, unknown numbers of women breathed freely again. Presumably their paramours, if still in town, did the same.

For a few weeks little was talked about except Mme. Restell's self-destruction. Then the rumor factories began to turn out fantastic tales. The abortionist was not dead at all. The body in the bathtub was that of a nameless woman destined for Potters Field. Mme. Restell, they whispered, had outwitted Comstock after all and was even now on the high seas, or already safe in Europe, her reticule heavy with gold bonds, the balance of her life pleasantly provided for by her illicit earnings. New Yorkers who had marveled at her past success in eluding the authorities preferred it this way. They had not liked Comstock's underhand trick, and found themselves wishing the rumors were true.

In fact, Mme. Restell was quite dead. The coroner had made sure of that, asking various persons to identify the body before shipping it off to the morgue. The woman who had begun her life in a little English shire town and made it one of danger, notoriety, and wealth had seen fit to end it herself. The experts who compiled such statistics would now have to pick another candidate for the title of "New York's most evil woman."

A humorous lithographer's rendering of "Fifth Avenue, Four Years after the Death of Madame Restell."

EPILOGUE

On the morning after the dramatic close of Mme. Restell's unusual career, the *New York Sun* voiced the sentiments of a large number of the city's inhabitants—possibly the majority of them. The writer shed no tears for the abortionist's death, but he excoriated Anthony Comstock for his tactics in trapping her:

> No matter what the wretched woman was who took her life with her own hand yesterday, her death has not freed the world from the last of detestable characters. Whatever she was, she had her rights and the man who cunningly led her into the commission of a misdemeanor acted an unmanly and ignoble part.
>
> The motive avowed by Mr. Comstock, according to the reports at the time, to wit, the vindication of his own character as a public prosecutor, afforded a poor apology for the meanness to which he stooped. He had been taunted, he said, with not daring to arrest her. So he deceived and wheedled her into a crime.

187

Everyone has rights. Even Anthony Comstock has his; but there is a healthier sentiment afloat today than usual, concerning the policy of doing evil that good may come, which he has seemed to be pursuing.

For many months the Restell case was a popular topic of conversation everywhere. Most people disliked Comstock's way of pursuing vice in the person of the late Mme. Restell. Many, thinking of her advanced age, felt that the law could have acted more leniently. More often discussed, but not so openly, was the question whether a woman had a right to decide not to have a baby.

And there were some who wondered if it would not have been wiser for Anna Trow Restell not to draw the blade across her throat, but to step out on her balcony over Fifth Avenue and cry out: "He that is without sin among you, let him first cast a stone."

SOURCES

ORIGINAL DOCUMENTS

Annual Reports of the Society for the Suppression of Vice.
Theodore Tilton *vs.* Henry Ward Beecher; Action for Criminal
Contempt. Tried in the City Court of Brooklyn. Verbatim
report in three volumes. New York. 1875.

PERIODICALS

Brooklyn Eagle
Leslie's Illustrated Weekly
National Police Gazette
New York Herald
New York Telegram
New York Times
Woodhull and Claflin's Weekly

PAMPHLETS

Huntington, Bishop. *Restell's Secret Life—A True History of
Her, from Birth to her Awful Death by her Own Wicked
Hands.* Philadelphia: Old Franklin Publishing House, 1897.
Tilton, Theodore. *Victoria C. Woodhull.* New York: Office of
Golden Age, 1871.

The Great Scandal—History of the Famous Beecher-Tilton Case. New York, 1874.

Trial of Caroline Lohman, alias Madame Restell. Reported verbatim for the *National Police Gazette* in the Court of General Sessions. New York. 1874.

BOOKS

Bennett, D. M. *Anthony Comstock: His Career of Cruelty and Crime.* New York: Da Capo Press, 1971.

Brown, Henry Collins. *Brownstone Fronts and Saratoga Trunks.* New York: Dutton, 1935.

Broun, Heywood, and Leech, Margaret. *Anthony Comstock; Roundsman of the Lord.* New York: Boni, 1927.

Comstock, Anthony. *Traps for the Young.* New York: Funk & Wagnalls, 1883.

Coon, Horace. *Columbia; Colossus on the Hudson.* New York: Dutton, 1947.

Doyle, J. E. P., comp. *Plymouth Church and its Pastor.* Hartford: Park Publishing Company, 1874.

Ellington, George. *The Women of New York.* New York: Arno Press, 1971; reprint of 1869 edition.

Hibben, Paxton. *Henry Ward Beecher: An American Portrait.* New York: Doran, 1927.

Johnston, Johanna. *Runaway to Heaven.* Garden City, N.Y.: Doubleday, 1963.

Jones, Edgar R. *Those Were the Good Old Days.* New York: Simon & Schuster, 1959.

Kouwenhoven, John A. *The Columbia Historical Portrait of New York.* Garden City, N.Y.: Doubleday, 1953.

Maurice, Arthur Bartlett. *Fifth Avenue.* New York: Dodd, Mead, 1918.

McCabe, James D., Jr. *Lights and Shadows of New York Life.* Philadelphia: National Publishing Company, 1872.

Morris, Lloyd. *Incredible New York.* New York: Random House, 1951.

Nevins, Allan, and Thomas, Milton Halsey, eds. *Diary of George Templeton Strong.* New York: Macmillan, 1952.

Sources

O'Connor, Richard. *Hell's Kitchen.* Philadelphia: Lippincott, 1958.

Phelps Stokes, I. N. *Iconography of Manhattan Island.* 5 vol. New York: R. H. Dowd, 1915–28.

Smith, Matthew Hale. *Sunshine and Shadow in New York.* Hartford: Burr & Co., 1868.

Still, Bayrd. *Mirror for Gotham.* New York: New York University Press, 1956.

Stowe, L. B. *Saints, Sinners and Beechers.* Indianapolis: Bobbs Merrill, 1934.

Cries of the Metropolis, or Humble Life in New York. Rutland Vt.: George A. Tuttle & Co., 1857.

Van Wyck, Frederick. *Recollections of an Old New Yorker.* New York: Liveright, 1932.

Werstein, Irving. *July, 1863.* New York: Julian Messner, 1957.

Wilson, Forrest. *Crusader in Crinoline.* Philadelphia: Lippincott, 1941

A prize-winning newspaper reporter, writer, editor and columnist, ALLAN KELLER worked for thirty-two years at the *World Telegram* and then the *World Journal Tribune* in New York City. He is the author of eight books of non-fiction previous to this one and has contributed articles to magazines ranging from the *Saturday Evening Post* to *American History, Illustrated.*

For twenty-three years Mr. Keller was a member of the faculty of the Graduate School of Journalism at Columbia University. He has lectured to publishing and editorial groups and has served as a panelist on television programs dealing with New York history, politics and government.

At present Mr. Keller lives in Darien, Connecticut, and serves as director of the James Gordon Bennett Memorial Foundation. He is married and the father of two grown daughters.